This book is dedicated with great affection and
respect to a wonderful colleague,
Professor Ethel Auster, 1942–2005.

# Messages, Meaning, and Symbols

## *The Communication of Information*

Charles T. Meadow

The Scarecrow Press, Inc.
Lanham, Maryland • Toronto • Oxford
2006

SCARECROW PRESS, INC.

Published in the United States of America
by Scarecrow Press, Inc.
A wholly owned subsidary of
The Rowman & Littlefield Publishing Group, Inc.
4501 Forbes Boulevard, Suite 200, Lanham, Maryland 20706
www.scarecrowpress.com

PO Box 317
Oxford
OX2 9RU, UK

British Library Cataloguing in Publication Information Available

**Library of Congress Cataloging-in-Publication Data**
Meadow, Charles T.
  Messages, meanings, and symbols : the communication of information /
Charles T. Meadow.
     p. cm.
  Includes bibliographical references and index.
  ISBN-13: 978-0-8108-5271-6 (pbk. : alk. paper)
  ISBN-10: 0-8108-5271-3 (pbk. : alk. paper)
  1. Communication. 2. Information theory. 3. Signs and symbols. I. Title.

P91.M3764 2006
302.2—dc22

                                    2005023069

# Contents

# Figures

# Preface

This book is about information, communication, and knowledge—what they are, how the communication of information increases knowledge, and the importance of communication in human, and even animal, life. These three terms have become overworked in our modern society but are of ever-increasing importance as we are surrounded, day and night, by *communications* media and often left to wonder if what we hear or see is *information*. Is it true? Is it meaningful? Does it fit with our existing *knowledge*? Does it expand our *knowledge*?

The emphasis in the book is on concepts and the meanings of these words. Communication includes print as well as electronic media, mass communication as well as person-to-person messaging, whether by mail, telephone, gesture, or e-mail. The book is *not* primarily about technology, the Internet, the World Wide Web, or e-mail, although all these are mentioned as important means of communication. It is about the fundamentals of information, recognizing that information science is little known and often little understood, and is concerned with how people exchange information and the fact that we do so in an amazing array of ways.

The assumed readers are undergraduates in information science and general readers, anyone from age fourteen or fifteen up. There is no required technical background, but there is an assumption that readers are willing to take a new look at some old ideas. The approach to concepts they hear much about but do not understand is often lighthearted, but it is serious in meaning. Obviously, technical explanations must be simplified to some extent, which may please the intended audience but not those who have advanced knowledge in the field.

I begin with a quick history of communication, mostly among humans, but never losing sight of the fact that animals also communicate and, according to some, so do plants. Humans have had the ability to communicate using symbols for far longer than we have had civilization, but during the lifetime of people reading this book we have seen enormous changes that we can better understand if we understand how we got to where we are today.

I then consider the nature of information, communication, and knowledge, not just how information is communicated, but what information, communication, and knowledge are. To convey information from one person to another (or animal or even ma-chine) we compose messages in which the information is represented by symbols. The symbols must have meaning. What is the meaning of *meaning*? What are the symbols we use? How is information transmitted? What are the media of transmission and what, in fact, are media? How do we communicate understanding, which is, after all, the usual point of communicating?

Next, I review the process of communication as a whole and wind up with a review of today's communication systems, their impact on us, and a hesitant look into the future (always a hazard, especially when technology is involved).

I have included many references to other works to provide more detail for the interested reader. In addition to these, there are excellent Web sites for many public and university libraries. Perhaps the best is the site of the Library of Congress catalog (http://catalog.loc.gov/), but be careful, many of the works listed are not easily available elsewhere. The citations at the end of each chapter are brief and refer to a full citation in the bibliography. I often cite the *Encyclopaedia Britannica*, an excellent general source for more information about most subjects. Because it exists in several different forms today—book, disk, and online—page references do not help much, so I have used only section or entry headings and listed them as "[insert the title here]in *Encyclopaedia Britannica*" Two other good general sources are *History of Tele-communications Technology, An Annotated Bibliography* by Sterling and Shiers, and *A History of Technology* edited by Singer and others, both fully cited in the bibliography. It is impossible to list all relevant work. An interested reader must do a lot of searching, on the Web and in libraries. Many people seem to feel that all the information they might want is on the Web and is free. Both assumptions are wrong. Just as in archaeology, there is no substitute for digging.

Numeric measures are given in metric units in a possibly vain hope to begin converting those still clinging to miles and yards. Years are identified as being the in Common Era (CE) or Before the Common Era (BCE), where the Common Era began in the year 1 of the nearly universal calendar.

Finally, the study of communication, information, and knowledge as one science is relatively new, but since everyone who can read and write knows and uses these three words at times, there are differences of opinion about what they mean and how they interrelate. We do get philosophical at times, delving into such questions as the meaning of *truth* and *meaning*. Of course, there are many points of view on these subjects. While I try to quote or cite other authors, in the final analysis I give my opinions in full recognition that they are not universally held.

---

I wish to acknowledge with gratitude the help of the following people: Sue Easun, Debra Meadow, and Mary Louise Meadow, editor-critics always with a great eye to improvement; Ron Ratsoy, an artist who knows how to present an idea; Al Tedesco, always ready with needed suggestions; Elizabeth (Bonnie) and Stephen Frick and Jinx Watson who read and made valuable suggestions on parts of the manuscript; Bradley Greenberg, for help on computer games; and Stephen Goring, Richard Friedman, and the American Museum of Radio and Electronics, for help with photos.

**1**

# History of Communication: Cave Drawing to Typewriters

Communication is based on the transmission of symbols and the interpretation of these symbols by the receiver of the communication. Symbols can be sounds, including spoken words or sounds from a horn, drum, or whistle; pictures, including the shapes we call letters and numerals; odors; tastes; and feelings (physical, not emotional). Some signals send emotional messages, but the emotion is in the mind of the sender and receiver, not in the signals. Although we stress human communication, we should never forget that we are not alone. Animals communicate by sound, gesture, odor, and touch. Some can receive messages that humans cannot detect, such as the strength and polarization of the earth's magnetic field. Even some plants are believed to communicate.

Humans were communicating long before they became civilized, that is, before farming, building towns, and doing specialized work. Some important technological inventions such as drawing and calendric notations came from quite primitive people. Writing, the alphabet, and an elegant notation for numbers came from early civilizations. Early Greeks used a code similar to Morse Code. Photography was experimented with in Egypt as early at the 8th century, although hardly successfully. The 18th-century French had a form of telegraph before electricity was harnessed.

An appreciation for how people have communicated throughout these centuries will better enable the reader to appreciate what the underlying concepts of communication are. Let's start with history—how communication began and developed, mainly among humans. In later chapters, I will analyze the basic concepts to better understand the ever-changing need for new means of communication and what it means to be an effective user of communications systems.

Communication is a vital part of life. Humans communicate from the womb before they are born. You have only to watch the faces of an expectant mother or father when they first feel the unborn child kick, to see that communication has taken place.

Generally, when we read history, we look for the names of the people who did important things—who invented something, who conquered someplace, who wrote what—and when. I try to provide that here, but often I don't even know who the first person was to invent something. What I do know is who did the most to bring the invention to the public, to make it widely used. Samuel F. B. Morse did not invent the electric telegraph, Alexander Graham Bell may not have invented the telephone, Guglielmo Marconi may not have invented radio, but these were the people who brought these inventions to practical reality. No one even tries to credit a single person with the invention of television.

The historical material is in mostly chronological order, but not exactly. It's also in order by the types of communication being discussed. So, in this chapter, I start with prehistoric communication and go all the way to the typewriter, a 19th-century invention.

But the typewriter is related to printing and printing to writing and writing was "invented" quite early in human history.

# The Very Beginning

How do we know when humans or animals first started communicating with each other? We do not know for sure. Some recorded messages date back tens of thousands of years. The use of symbols for words came much later. Humans, or beings something like humans, have been around for millions of years. Our own species, *Homo sapiens*, meaning wise man or person, is about 200,000 years old. Even before we became wise, our ancestors could communicate by gestures and grunts or other primitive noises, more or less as animals do today. If we take the Bible literally then the first man, Adam, conversed with God and Eve in a fully developed language right from the start.

The more archeologists dig in various parts of the world, the more evidence they find of early drawings, writings, and musical instruments. When people write the history of their own culture and technology, they tend to include only what affected their culture. If an invention was made in Korea but never brought into Middle Eastern, European, or American culture, we don't give it much attention. Take movable type printing, for example. This is a means of printing in which each letter or symbol is on an individual piece of type. The pieces of type are assembled into words and sentences as needed. When a full page is set, it can be printed and then the pieces of type saved for the next use. We credit Johannes Gutenberg with the invention. He built the first European movable type press in Germany and there is no evidence that he ever heard that the Koreans had invented it first.

Drawings about 50,000 years old have been recovered from caves in what are now France and Spain. Careful study has shown that these are not simply pictures of animals, the usual main subjects, but messages. They appear to portray a kind of religious ritual, especially the killing or sacrificing of an animal. At least one included marks that appear to tell when this ritual killing should be, or was, performed (see figure 1.1). These drawings and markings are certainly a form of recorded communication and might be considered the earliest writing. But as far as we know, they did not come directly into any of the cultures of the modern world. Writing in Indo-European languages developed much later, in other cultures.

How did speech develop? Some believe it started as imitation of animal sounds, some that it developed in imitation of the sound of primitive musical instruments, and some simply that our own grunts became ever more varied and complex and slowly became speech. Surely, no one person invented the concept of a word. Words would have evolved by repeating sounds made when facing danger, pointing to food, or seeking to impress a possible mate. Much of animal communication is based on mating rituals and this makes it more likely that pre-*Homo sapiens* peoples could communicate at some level about such an important matter. The peacock showing off his colorful tail is an example. He's not showing off to zoo visitors, he's showing off to the peahen of his choice (see figure 1.2).

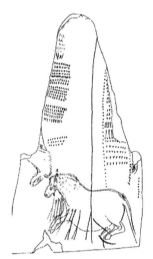

Figure 1.1. *Drawing carved on a bone found in a cave in France.* This drawing, which dates from 20,000 to 40,000 years ago, depicts a pregnant mare being ritually killed. The lines pointing to her body represent spears or darts. The smaller shapes in tabular form are believed to be used for determining when this ceremony was carried out or should next be carried out. Drawing courtesy of Alexander Marshack, *The Roots of Civilization.*

Figure 1.2. *A peacock "presenting."* This display of finery is intended to impress peahens, the females of the species. To us it is a beautiful sight; to them it has a very specific meaning.

# Writing

The earliest known writing that is related to our own writing was developed either in Sumer, Egypt, or what is now Pakistan. Sumer was a tiny nation located between the Tigris and Euphrates rivers in what is present-day Iraq. By writing, we usually mean symbols recorded on a flat surface. Before Sumerians learned to do that, they made three-dimensional symbols or tokens out of clay. Some examples date from as early as 3300 BCE (see figure 1.3). These were to represent goods exchanged in trade—perhaps the delivery of ten goats—to be paid for later. In this case, ten goat tokens would be formed and exchanged for the real goats, as a promise to pay later. Then an envelope came into use to hold the tokens, the envelope being a clay box. Still later, Sumerians and others in the region began to make a picture of the symbols that were inside the box and inscribe them on the outside so the contents could easily be known. And later still someone thought, *Well, why bother with the three-dimensional shapes? I can just make two-dimensional marks on a flat piece of clay; that will say the same thing but be easier for all concerned to make, carry, and store.* This form of image writing came about 3000 BCE (see figure 1.4). Of course, it wasn't done by one person, all at once. It took time to evolve. All these dates are approximate.

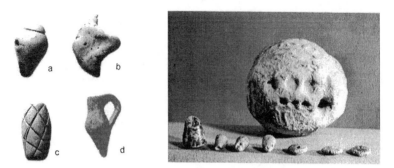

Figure 1.3. *Tokens, typically representing objects in trade, and a containing envelope.* A token might represent a sheep or a quantity of grain. Some of these, shown at left, were found in Iraq. Symbol a represents a unit of oil, its shape being that of a typical oil container of the times. The next, b, represents a cow though it takes a bit of imagination to see the animal. A unit of string is portrayed in c, resembling a modern-day cone of string. Finally, d represents a unit of sheep's milk in a pitcher. These were found in Uruk, Iraq. Courtesy Vorderasiatisches Museum, Berlin, Germany (Bodestrasse 1-3, D-1020) and Professor Denise Schmandt-Besserat. At right, in the foreground, are some tokens resembling those on the left. Behind them is an "envelope" that might have contained them, with some impressions of the tokens on the outside. These are from Susa, Iran, dated around 3300 BCE. Courtesy of Musée du Louvre, Départment Antiquités Orientales and Professor Denise Schmandt-Besserat.

Figure 1.4. *Pictographic symbols, the written versions of the tokens.* The circular signs at the top indicate large measures of grain, the wedge shapes smaller measures. They are "written" on a flat piece of clay. Courtesy of Cuyler Young Jr., Royal Ontario Museum, Toronto, and Professor Denise Schmandt-Besserat.

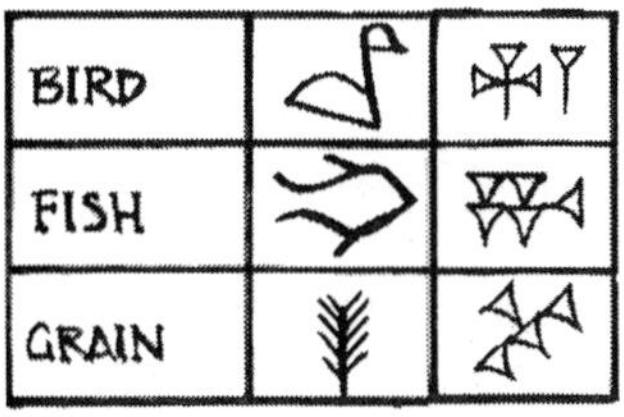

| | | |
|---|---|---|
| BIRD | | |
| FISH | | |
| GRAIN | | |

Figure 1.5. *Written symbols.* Symbols resembling the earlier three-dimensional images (l.) and those written in newer cuneiform (r.). Cuneiform required only one basic symbol, the line and arrow head, although it could occur in different lengths and orientations and in combinations with other basic symbols.

And so, humans learned to write. At first, each symbol represented one thing and there would have been a spoken equivalent—that is, a word for goat, another for bird. The written symbol would have had some resemblance to what it stood for.

Gradually, writing became streamlined, and instead of this pictorial writing a new form of notation was invented—cuneiform (see figure 1.5). The new symbols were made of two parts, a triangle and a sort of tail. The tail could vary in length and the whole thing could point in any direction. A word would consist of several of these elements, so there was still one picture-like symbol for each word, but all the symbols were made up from repetitions of the same basic component. The complete symbol no longer looked like what it represented—just as our words do not. The letter-symbol "horse" does not look anything like the animal. The use of a smaller number of basic symbols simplified the act of writing. A scribe did not have to be an artist, but he did have to learn a great many symbols. Both Egyptian hieroglyphics and Chinese writing, called pictographic or ideographic, use picture-like symbols to represent words, sounds, or to modify the meaning of other symbols. Figure 1.6 shows an example of writing in modern Mandarin, the principal language of modern China. Although this language handles such concepts as plurals and verb tenses differently from English, the meanings do get across. The symbols used do not look to us much like what they represent, but consider how much stellar constellations really resemble the gods and animals "clearly"seen by the ancients.

Writing was not only a technical convenience for recording messages, it also achieved great emotional value. Laws and religious teachings began to be put in written form. Both the Hebrew and Christian scriptures, once existing only in oral form, became holy items when written; not just their content, but the written objects themselves. Moslems sometimes refer to both Christians and Jews as the People of the Book because Islam accepts the basic teachings of both bibles. Today, a written law, contract, or treaty usually takes precedence over an oral agreement, and libel (written defamation) carries a higher penalty than slander—the oral form of the same offense.

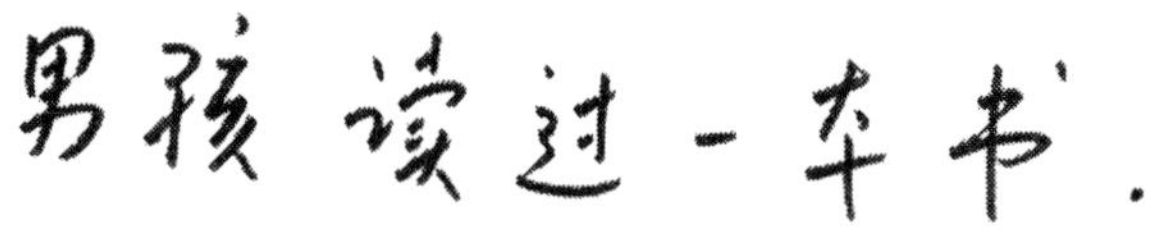

男孩 读过 - 本书.

Figure 1.6. *Mandarin writing*. The first two characters indicate a male boy. The third means *read* and the fourth says that the preceding sign refers to the past. The next two signs together mean *one* or *a*, and the last means *book*. Hence, "The boy has read the book." Courtesy of Dr. Lauren Dong.

## What to Write On

Inventing the symbols and how to use them is one thing. But if writing was to be really successful, it had to be relatively easy to *do* the writing and it would certainly help if the written text could be easily moved or stored. Also, since we all make mistakes, it would be nice to be able to correct an error. The first writing material, in Sumer, was clay. While still soft, clay can easily be written on and a mistake could easily be corrected. Once it hardened, though, correction or an addition to the same tablet was out of the question. Another advantage of clay is that it lasts. Many ancient clay tablets have survived for thousands of years.

Putting together a book-length clay document or carrying one on a trip would be quite a challenge. What else was available? In Egypt, a reed plant called *papyrus* grew in the Nile River. Its stem contained a pulpy material, which could be mashed, flattened into strips, woven into sheets, and dried to produce something like our modern paper. However, there was only a limited amount of papyrus and the Egyptians were not eager to share it with other peoples.

Another alternative to clay was animal skin. Skins were cleaned and scraped smooth, providing a writing surface that was lightweight, longer lasting than papyrus, and erasable. One form made from sheepskin was called *parchment* in English, a word derived from Pergamum, a city in what is now Turkey, where this material was first used. If an error was made, a scribe could scrape off ink with a knife and rewrite the offending part. Another form of animal skin, *vellum*, was made from calfskin, which required more processing than sheepskin. The word *vellum* is related to our word *veal*, referring to a calf or meat of the calf. Both of these names for writing material are still used today. Sheepskin may refer to a college diploma, once actually written on parchment but now on paper. Vellum now refers to several varieties of fine paper that are no longer made from skins.

What about ink? Yes, ink had to be invented, too. There were many materials that could be used to make legible marks on papyrus or parchment, such as berry juice or soft stones, but for most purposes an ink that would not easily smear or fade away was needed. The markings had to remain visible for a very long time. Ink was in use as far back as 2500 BCE when it would have been used on papyrus or cloth. This early ink consisted of some form of powdered carbon and another usually oily substance to bind the carbon to the writing surface. Water would be added just before use. The carbon could come from pulverizing charcoal or from the tiny particles of pure carbon that form on the chimney of a hurricane lamp or lantern as the fuel burns. Later, other chemicals, such as liquids squeezed from some tree barks or betel nuts, were used.

Papyrus and parchment were in short supply as writing and therefore documents became more popular. In China, Tsai Lun invented a new writing substance now called *paper* around the year 100 CE. Originally, paper was made from the pulp of wood bark to which might be added bits of hemp waste, old rags, even old fish nets. These were pounded until all that remained was a mash of fibers. Today, most paper is made from wood pulp but can also be made from cloth fibers, or the two can be mixed to provide high-quality, wood-based paper. The Chinese process of papermaking was kept secret at first, but during a war in Samarkand in modern-day Uzbekistan along the Silk Road between East Asia and Europe, some Chinese papermakers were captured and the secret came out to the West. This was in 751 CE. The process remained in the Islamic world for some time and gradually spread to Europe via Spain, then largely an Islamic country. The first European paper mill was opened around 1100. By that time, the production of papyrus had nearly stopped, making paper more valuable. If paper is well made it is as good as papyrus as a writing medium and more durable. It is far cheaper to manufacture than animal skins. If made from cloth, it can last almost as long as skins; some of our museums and libraries still have some of the earliest books ever printed on paper.

# The Alphabet and Numbers

When did someone get the idea that instead of representing a word with a set of cuneiform marks, it could be represented by a symbol for each sound that made up the spoken word? Once again, it is not likely that the idea for this system of writing came all at once to one person. It surely evolved over many years, but it's kind of fun to imagine one person jumping up and shouting, "Eureka!" as the alphabet was born.

The idea of an alphabet is that symbols called letters represent sounds rather than objects or concepts. Several letters strung together, or sometimes even a single one, can stand for a single concept and can tell a reader how to pronounce the word. That means that if you know how to pronounce a word, you can know, at least approximately, how to spell it. If you see it written, you know, at least approximately, how to pronounce it. Many fewer symbols need to be learned with an alphabet compared to a pictorial system of writing, although there may be the same number of words in use. This made it easier to learn to be a scribe, hence more people learned to read and write than could by using hieroglyphics or cuneiform. It made it easier to keep records, write laws, describe things and people, and record stories. It became perhaps the most powerful means of recording thought that people had ever developed.

Use of an alphabet lets us get by with just a few basic symbols. In English we have 26 letters, 52 if you count both lower case and capitals. Then there are punctuation symbols, 32 on my computer keyboard, ` ~ ! @ # $ % ^ & * ( ) - _ = + [ ] { } \ | ; : ' " , < . > / ? and there has to be a blank or space to show where one word ends and another begins. Still, that's not too many. Where schooling is good, most children have learned the alphabet by about age six and the punctuation symbols a few years later.

The alphabet we use derives from one (or more) that originated among Semitic peoples who lived in Akkadia (or Phoenicia, or roughly modern-day Lebanon), present-day Israel and Palestine, and Egypt. Wherever it started, people in this region appear to have been the first to use an alphabet. They were a seafaring and trading people, and some lived in Egypt as either laborers or captives. The new idea of how to write spread quickly and eventually evolved into the Hebrew and Arabic alphabets. Both originally got along without vowels. The reader would see a string of consonants and was expected to understand from the context what vowel sounds were needed. More than one spoken word could be represented by one string of consonants. In the modern versions of these lang-uages, extra marks above or below a letter indicate what vowel sounds are needed. Figure 1.7. shows an example taken from the book of Deuteronomy (25:19). It tells of instructions given to Moses while the Hebrews were wandering in the Sinai desert and were harassed by the Amalekites, who were led by a man named

Amalek. The sentence illustrated can be interpreted as a command to erase the memory of Amalek. It can also be interpreted as a command to eliminate his male followers—quite a different meaning. *Ths wrks smwht n nglsh s wll.*

לְרִשְׁתָּה תִּמְחֶה אֶת־זֵכֶר עֲמָלֵק
מִתַּחַת הַשָּׁמָיִם לֹא תִּשְׁכָּח: פפפ

Figure 1.7. *Hebrew writing.* The basic language has no vowels. Instead, marks above and below the letters were devised to provide them but are not always used, even in modern times. If not, there is always uncertainty as to what words are represented, to be resolved by context. The text above means either *eliminate the memory of Amelek*, or, linguistically similar but hugely different in terms of action to be taken, *eliminate his followers.* Courtesy of Rabbi Norman Berlat.

The original alphabet eventually spread to Greece, and it was the Greeks who added vowels and spread the new invention throughout Europe. In western Europe it became the Latin alphabet used in slightly different forms for English, French, Spanish, Portuguese, Roumanian, and several Slavic languages such as Polish and Czech. In eastern Europe, it took the form of the Cyrillic alphabet used in Russia and several counties bordering it. Our English alphabet, derived from Latin, has 26 letters, Greek has 24, and Russian has 32. Our word *alphabet* comes from the names of the first two letters of the Greek alphabet, *alpha* and *beta*.

Did the alphabet make any real difference in the world? Most scholars say yes. At the very least, it helped spread knowledge of reading and writing, which, in turn, led to the development of literature, religion, science, and commerce. Some feel that this form of writing and representing thought led to the development of theoretical science rather than merely technology. Theoretical science studies the nature of substances or actions and formulates rules governing them. Technology is concerned with making practical tools to accomplish tasks. Ancient China, where art, government, and technology had flourished, did not develop basic science as we know it today. This happened first in the Islamic world and then in Europe. Many scholars say that people who become used to reading and writing in a linear (straight line) fashion following strict rules for composition began to think in terms of abstract rules. Does this imply that Mid-Easterners and Europeans are better or smarter than Chinese? Certainly not—just different in some ways. The alphabet may have been the main cause of the difference.

Plato offered another view not just of the alphabet but of all writing. He attributed the words to Socrates having him quote an Egyptian pharaoh, speaking to the god who invented writing, "[Y]our invention will produce forgetfulness in the souls of those who have learned it, through lack of practice at using their memory, as through reliance on writing they are reminded from outside by alien marks, not from inside, themselves by themselves: you have discovered an elixir not of memory but of reminding. To your students you give an appearance of wisdom not the reality of it. . . ."[1]

Numbers also became simplified. What we call Arabic numerals originated in India and, like printing and other technologies, worked their way west, first into the Islamic world—hence the name we still use—and then into the Western world. This system has the zero and the decimal point, which enable us to represent fractions (values less than one) in our numbering system and greatly simplifies calculations.

The zero is an interesting symbol. What does it mean? Nothing. Yes, it means something, but what it means is *nothing*. Why do we need a symbol to mean nothing? It helps us understand other symbols and gives us a notation for mathematics that has been important for all sciences. We still use Roman numerals, mostly for clocks and numbering things like Superbowls. We know that XII is twelve and IV is four and the sum is XVI. But how do we add these numerals? Not column by column. How do we multiply them? How much is IX times VI?[2]

The numeral system we use today is based on Arabic numerals and makes arithmetic much easier because we can add or multiply column by column. Our symbols for numbers show how many ones, how many tens, how many hundreds, and so on, are combined in any number. The number 123 means one hundred, two tens, and three ones. The number 2.86 means two ones, eight tenths, and six hundredths. What about 103? That means one hundred and three ones, with no, or zero, tens. Without the ability to symbolize that there are no tens in one hundred three we might be stuck with a numeric symbol system as cumbersome as Roman numerals and therefore could not use the position of a digit to indicate its value. We need a way to show "nothing." We cannot say science would be impossible without such a numbering system, but it would be harder to learn and harder to do calculations, hence science would have been slower to develop.

# Printing

During the Middle Ages, about 500 to 1500 CE, classical European learning was not widely disseminated in Europe but was supported by the Christian Church. In the 14th century European civilization entered the Renaissance, which meant that classical culture was reborn, bringing back art and learning. More people became interested in reading and thinking for themselves. In the 16th century the Reformation, or reforming of the established church, again led to more ordinary people reading and thinking independently.

By the 15th century Europe had paper, a hunger for reading, and a new means of printing. The result was a great demand for printed books. In 1454 (the commonly assumed year), Johannes Gutenberg created a new kind of press that required each letter, number, or other symbol to be carved into a separate piece of metal, or type. The pieces were stored in type cases. To print a line of text, the printer drew types from a case and arranged them in the order needed to represent the text. Then another line was set, and so on. When a complete page was set up, it could be printed again and again, after which the types were resorted back into the cases and made ready to be used again on a different page. This form of printing is still occasionally used today. While slow compared to modern computer word processors and printers, it is far faster at making multiple copies than making each copy by hand.

One challenge for Gutenberg was to make typefaces where each piece of type was of exactly the same height. There was no mass production or automatic machine tool to do this. The type faces were cast—formed by pouring molten metal into a form. This required great skill by the workers. Gutenberg was a goldsmith, so he was used to precise metal work.

Ink was another challenge. One kind of ink works well when the writing surface is paper or paperlike and the means of applying ink to the surface is a pen, brush, or wood used for block printing. For printing with metal type, Gutenberg had to come up with an ink that had just the right ability to stick to metal yet would come off easily when paper was pressed against the inked metal. He had to solve both these problems himself or find someone who could. He certainly could not look up ink suppliers in the Yellow Pages.

Printing has come a long way since Gutenberg. Figure 1.8 shows a letterpress, a form of press more like Gutenberg's than modern printers, but still occasionally in use today. Figure 1.9 shows a modern newspaper printing plant and figure 1.10 shows a typical printer used with a computer.

Some feel fewer books are being published today because of computers, movies, and television, but this is not so. Figure 1.11 shows the number of books produced per year worldwide and in the United States since Gutenberg's day. Books, newspapers, and magazines remain important means of communication over most of the world even today. It is interesting that the use of computers, long predicted to replace paper, has actually increased its use for printouts and multiple copies of documents.[3]

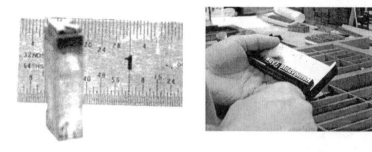

a                                          b

c                                          d

Figure 1.8. *Typesetting and printing by letterpress.* This form of printing is basically the same as that used by Gutenberg, except that paper is fed and inking done automatically. These presses, still found in use today, require the printer to select a typeface (a) for each letter, assemble lines of type into a *stick* (b), then assemble the contents of several sticks into a case (c). The case is fixed onto the printer (d) and inked from the large, round plate, which is in turn inked by a roller in position at the top of the plate. Printing a modern newspaper, considering its size and number of copies, would be virtually impossible by this means. Photos by the author. Printing equipment courtesy of Stephen Goring.

Figure 1.9. *Printing a modern newspaper. The Knoxville* (Tenn.) *News Sentinel* press is larger than many buildings. It is seven stories high and can print 70,000 copies of the full paper per hour. Note the life-size figure of Santa Claus (arrow) for comparison. The press is fed from a huge roll of paper called a *web* and it can print pages sequentially, cut the pages, assemble, and fold the complete paper. Printing of advertising leaflets or the pages for a small, limited-edition book is possible but would be prohibitively expensive on such a machine. Photo courtesy *The Knoxville News Sentinel.*

Figure 1.10. *A modern computer printer.* This performs all the functions of a letterpress but mostly automatically. The user tells the computer to select the file to be printed and the desired typeface and then tells the printer to start. The printer's ink or toner is in a cartridge provided by the user and makes the appropriate marks on the page. Its speed is greater than that of a letterpress but much slower than that of newspaper presses. This printer was used to prepare the pages of this book. Photo by the author.

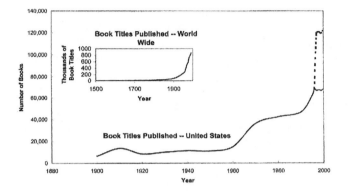

Figure 1.11. *Graph of book publication.* The main graph shows the number of titles (not number of copies) published in the United States from 1900 to 2004. The inset shows worldwide publication. It can be seen that books are being published at a rate that has been generally increasing since printing began. In 1997 a new method of compiling these data came into use and this produced figures about 1.8 times as high as had previously been estimated. From that date on two curves, representing the two approaches, are shown in the figure. The truth probably lies somewhere between them. Note the sharp increase in 2004.[4]

# The Typewriter

The next most important development in mechanized printing after Gutenberg was likely the typewriter, first patented in the United States in 1868. Printing presses, of course, had been improved since 1454, but the typewriter brought mechanical printing into the office and eventually into the home.

For those who may never have used one, a typewriter consists of a keyboard; a set of hammers each containing the image of a letter or other symbol; a platen or roller with some controls to move it; a movable carriage holding the platen; and a ribbon saturated with ink (see figure 1.12). Each key on the keyboard is linked to a single hammer so that striking that key causes the corresponding hammer to strike the ribbon, press it against the paper, and thereby imprint the character. In a computer, striking a key causes the corresponding letter to be displayed on the screen. After each typewriter key strike, the carriage moves the width of one character to the left so each character goes to the right of the preceding one. A computer simply moves a cursor, not the whole screen. At the end of a line on the typewriter, the operator hits a lever that moves the whole carriage, platen, and paper back to the left side of the next line. Both operations, line feed and carriage return, can be done by pressing a lever. A computer word processor does both steps automatically.

Today, mechanical typewriter workings seem primitive. It is, but for its time it was a great accomplishment, enabling good, clear text to be produced and a few copies to be made at the same time as the original using something called carbon paper.

Figure 1.12. *A typewriter from the early 20th century.* As with a computer printer, the user selects a typeface by striking a key on the keyboard, which is linked to a hammer containing the image of the symbol (letter, numeral, or punctuation sign). Between the image and the paper is an inked ribbon. As the hammer hits the ribbon, an inked copy of the symbol is impressed on the page. By comparison, a computer keyboard sends an electronic message to the computer indicating what symbol to print. In the early days there was no choice of font, but in the second half of the century electric typewriters often allowed for such changes to be made easily. Photo by the author.

The typewriter quickly spread to offices. Mark Twain is believed to have been the first author ever to submit a typewritten manuscript to a publisher. In 1884 Ottmar Merganthaler invented what looked like a giant typewriter, called the Linotype. Instead of printing on paper, it produced complete lines of metal type, which were then used to print newspapers or books—a great saving in production time. The type was created in the machine from molten metal, which was melted and used again (see figure 1.13).

Figure 1.13. *A Linotype machine and some lines of type it produced.* This is a large machine, about as tall as an average person. The operation used a keyboard similar to that of the type-writer. Instead of making impressions on a page, the Linotype poured molten metal into a mold for the selected letter and justified each line as it was completed. The resulting lines could be used on a letterpress or newspaper press. The metal was easily reclaimed and reused. Photo courtesy of Heildelberg Canada.

In the 20th century portable typewriters were available and became common in homes. Many college students had their own because instructors began to insist on typewritten essays. In the 1950s electric typewriters were produced. These enabled a skilled typist to type faster using less physical effort. Today, the typeriter has become a word processor and the software to run it is found in most computers—it is no longer a separate machine.

If you want to buy a typewriter today you would probably have to look for it in an antique store rather than at an office supply store. To see the ultimate in printing machines, try to get a tour of your local newspaper's printing plant.

---

Humans took an unknown number of years to develop true speech, that is, use of words and grammar to combine words. It probably took millions of years to do this. An early form of writing represented words with pictures. From there to the alphabet took perhaps only five thousand years. From the alphabet to printing in the modern sense took about another five thousand years, bringing us to about the year 1454. It was four hundred years later that the electric telegraph was invented. Since then, progress has been simply dazzling. We'll now describe what happened during those four hundred pre-electronic years.

## Notes

1. Plato. *Phaedrus*, p. 123.
2. "Mathematics, History of" in *Encyclopaedia Britannica*.
3. Sellen and Harper, *The Myth of the Paperless Office*.
4. These data are from: *UNESCO Statistical Yearbook;* Kurian, *Datapedia*; *Statistical Abstract of the United States*.

## Further Reading

### General

Crowley and Heyer. *Communication in History.*
Meadow. *Ink into Bits.*

————. *Making Connections.*
Solymar. *Getting the Message.*
Sterling and Shiers. *History of Telecommunications Technology.*
Warner. *From Writing to Computers.*
————. *Information, Knowledge, Text.*

## The Very Beginning

Altmann. *The Ascent of Babel.*
Boorstin. *The Discoverers:* 480-556.
Crowley and Heyer. *Communication in History.* The whole of "Part I, The Media of Early Civilization," pp. 1–42, which includes the Marshack and Schmandt-Besserat articles listed below.
"'Earliest Writing' Found" (Web site).
"First Alphabet Found in Egypt" (Web site).
Marshack. "The Art and Symbols of Ice Age Man."
————. *The Roots of Civilization.*
Ong. "Orality, Literacy, and Modern Media."
Schmandt-Besserat. "The Earliest Precursor of Writing."
Wilford, "A is for Ancient, Describing an Alphabet Found Near Jerusalem" (Web site).
————. "Who Began Writing?" (Web site).

## Language

Baker. *The Atoms of Language.*
Chomsky. *On Nature and Language.*
Pinker. *The Language Instinct.*
Ruhlen. *The Origin of Language.*
Yule. *The Study of Language.*

## Writing and Reading

Illich. *In the Vineyard of the Text.*
Kilgour. *The Evolution of the Book.* Chapter 2, "Incunables on Clay," pp. 11–21 and Chapter 3, "Papyrus Rolls," pp. 22–33.
Manguel. *A History of Reading.*
Nunberg. *The Future of the Book.*
Robinson. "The Origins of Writing."

Schmandt-Besserat. "The Earliest Precursor of Writing."
Ullman. *Ancient Writing and Its Influence.*

## Writing Materials and Ink

Carvalho. *Forty Centuries of Ink.*
Finley. *Printing Paper and Ink.*
Hunter. *Papermaking.*

## The Alphabet and Numbers

Ifrah. *From One to Zero, A Universal History of Numbers.*
Logan. *The Alphabet Effect.*
————. *The Fifth Language.*
Man. *Alpha Beta.*
Pinker. *The Language Instinct.*
Sacks. *Language Visible.*
Shlain. *The Alphabet Versus the Goddess.*
Yule. *The Study of Language.*

## Printing

Behrman. *The Remarkable Writing Machine.*
Chappell and Bringhurst. *A Short History of the Printed Word.*
Eisenstein. *The Printing Press as an Agent of Change.*
Kilgour. *The Evolution of the Book.*
Linoff. *The Typewriter.*
Mares. *The History of the Typewriter.*
Mumford. *The Print Revolution.*
"A Timeline History of the IBM Typewriter."
Twain. "The First Writing Machines" (Web site).

**2**

# History of Communication: Sound, Light, and Transportation

The earliest channels of communication include those still commonly used today: light, in the fork of waves that can carry images, and sound, in the form of waves that could travel through air (see box, p. 26), carrying voices and other noises. Our earliest ancestors would have used these. What we humans added was greater variation in how the sounds and images were formed and transmitted than lower animals were able to do. There was one other mode of transmission used quite early—transporting the message if recorded, or transporting a person who delivered the message "recorded" in his mind.

From the time Gutenberg's movable-type printing press was invented in 1454 until the electric telegraph came along in 1837 (in England) or 1844 (in the United States), roughly four hundred years passed. During this time America was "discovered" and heavily settled by Europeans, and modern European states developed. Trade between the West and Asian countries had already been underway for many years. The East-West trade route was along what became known as the Silk Road and had been established since the 2nd century BCE, but activity vastly increased as means of transportation improved. Along with travel go messages and trade. Messages could be formal letters from one king or merchant to another, or exchange of cultural ideas by casual conversation between the travelers and the locals. Formal or not, it was all communication. Marco Polo, for example, traveled from Venice over much of Asia, visiting many kingdoms that had different customs and languages and was able to communicate wherever he went.[1]

Arthur C. Clarke, the man who first conceived of the communications satellite (see chapter 4), wrote, "When Queen Victoria came to the throne in 1837, she had no swifter means of sending messages to the far parts of her empire than had Julius Caesar—or, for that matter, Moses."[2] This is not quite accurate. Victoria's ships were capable of traveling longer distances than Caesar's and had better navigational instruments, which meant ships were more likely to get to their destination and do it safely. Much earlier, Moses didn't need ships. He had another way of crossing the Red Sea. Pretty much all the nontransportation advances in communication that were made in the Moses-to-Victoria period were in the form of recording media, mainly the printing press (described in the previous chapter) and photography (described in the next chapter). During Victoria's long reign, which ended in 1901, electricity came into use for powering the telegraph, the telephone, and illumination lamps.

Historians Allan Nevins and Henry Steele Commager suggest that the creation of an Electoral College to select the President of the United States rather than direct election was at least partially due to the inability of Americans to communicate throughout their new country when the Constitution was adopted.[3] The time required to collect ballots from a widely distributed population would be bad enough. The problem of getting information about candidates to these people would make the whole process impractical.

Here and in the next two chapters we introduce some technical terms. Mostly, they are defined or discussed in a side bar or box.

## Sound Transmission

Early people had done a great deal with sound by using mechanical devices to increase the distance a message could travel compared to the range of the human voice. Basically, these were drums and horns or pipes, which are still used today. One good example of early mes-sage transmission by sound was the use of drums in Africa (see figure 2.1). We don't know exactly when this began, but they were found in use in the 18th century when European explorers began to move beyond the coastal settlements. Large drums make deep (low-frequency) sounds, which travel far in forested areas. (See box, p. 28) Drums cannot make much variation in sound; however, if you hit the drum head with a stick near its center you get a low note; if you hit nearer the edge you get a higher note.

At least one tribe found they could send whole sentences with the drum. They used different beats to correspond with the emphasized syllables in a sentence. Take the modern-day sentence

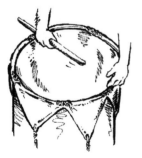

Figure 2.1. *Drums for signaling.* Over the right terrain, the sounds made by drums can carry quite far. The messages must be encoded. Some of the most effective were found in use in Africa when European explorers first went there. Like alphabetic writing without vowels, the messages could be ambiguous but worked well.

"I want to go to the game." One way to say this is to stress the words *want*, *go*, and *game*. I *want* to *go* to the *game*. The drum beat sequence would be a light or higher frequency tap, then a heavy or low-frequency tap, another high and a low, then two high ones, and finally a low one.

At this point you should be thinking, "Wait a minute, there are other sentences that might be stressed the same way. How does the recipient know which words you were sending?" The answer: they may not. Recipients had to know roughly what the topic was in order to understand the message. I will say more about this in chapter 6. But the method worked. European observers were surprised by and impressed with this effective use of a drum.[4]

***Sound waves*** are a series of vibrations or alternating compressions and expansions of air or some other medium. The waves can also travel through other media such as wood, metal, the head of a drum, the strings of a violin, or the reeds in an oboe or clarinet. Waves can vary in their height (amplitude), length, and frequency. Our ears contain small drums that are vibrated by sound waves and then send signals to our brains telling what was heard. Compression? Expansion? Yes. The amount of compression and expansion is very slight, so you may not be aware of it. But if you lay a finger lightly on the a piano as someone hits the keys, you can feel the vibrations. You can see waves in water, the alternate raising and lowering of the level of water in anything from the bathtub to the ocean. The *frequency* of any waves is the number of them generated per second. Frequency is measured in *hertz*. One hertz means one wave cycle (starting up, reaching peak, going down, then returning to starting position) per second. One kilohertz means one thousand waves per second. Humans can hear sound only in a certain range, about 20 to 20,000 cycles per second, or 20 to 20,000 hertz. This varies a great deal from person to person. The frequency of ocean waves will normally be less than one hertz, roughly one wave every two or five seconds. The speed of sound varies with the medium. In air at sea level (air higher up is thinner) sound travels at 331 meters per second or 1,089 feet per second. In water at 8°C the speed is 1,429 meters per second.

Other uses of sound signals commonly found today are whistles, horns (bugles to tell soldiers or sailors what to do), bells, snapping of fingers, or just saying "Ahem" to get someone's attention. Very low-frequency sound waves—lower than that of large drums and below the level that humans can hear—are made by such natural forces as the rumbling before an earthquake. Scientists have developed ways to use these waves to detect avalanches, tornadoes, and even meteors entering the Earth's atmosphere. These, of course, are not intentional messages, but they do convey information.

Let us go back to the situation quoted at the start of this chapter. Just about all major improvements in long-range communications from roughly the time of Caesar to the beginning of Queen Victoria's reign were in transportation. Our channels for *carrying* messages got better and better. Our channels for direct transmission by light or sound did not change much. Of course, the printing press was a great help in communication, but its products—books—had to be transported in order to reach more than a few people. Around the beginning of the 19th century we harnessed steam power for use in transportation. Railways (whose locomotives were once called "iron horses") and ships made enormous differences in our ability to communicate. Figure 2.2 shows a sequence of trains from the *Tom Thumb*, first passenger locomotive used in the United States (1830) to today's high-speed Japanese "bullet train," the *Shinkansen*.

# Light

Light has been in existence since the beginning of the universe. In the earliest days of human existence it served only to enable the receipt of information, allowing our human predecessors to see their environment. Later it served to transmit gestures as well as to receive them. Inevitably, our ancestors learned to codify gestures (see chapter 5) just as they codified sounds into language. Eventually, technology was used to send signals via light, first the use of

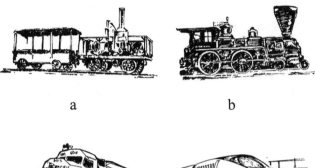

a                                    b

c                              d

Figure 2.2. *Development of trains.* Here are: (a) the earliest steam locomotive used in the United States, called *Tom Thumb* and operated from 1830 by the Chesapeake and Ohio Railroad. Dirty and slow by our standards, these came to revolutionize ground transportation, and therefore communication. In the mid-19th century, locomotives had evolved into that at b; in the mid-20th century to that shown at c, a type still in use. At d is one of the Japanese bullet trains, among the fastest in the world at 300 kilometers per hour (180 mph).

fire to send messages at night and smoke to do so in daylight. In early Greek and Roman civilization, beginning about 500 BCE, identification symbols such as flags and badges were used in war to identify army units or ships. Today, of course, we have electric light traffic signals, neon signs carrying commercial messages, and icons on our computer screens. And we have the basic electric light that can enable us to read the printed word or can be used to show us our way in the dark. Is this a communications medium? Light brings us messages. As Marshall McLuhan said, "The instance of the electric light may prove illuminating in this connection. The electric light is pure information. It is a medium without a message, as it were, unless it is used to spell out some verbal ad."[5] Note that the use of light for signaling, as in sending Morse code messages from one ship at sea to another, means that light is the carrier or channel for the message, not its content, as illumination is when it makes it possible to see a message recorded by another medium, as an advertising billboard or your book at night.

## Mail

Once writing was developed, the concept of mail followed. This means sending (transmitting) written messages, typically over long distances. The first known organized mail service was developed in Egypt around 2000 BCE. Its progress was largely the progress of transportation, at first on the backs of animals, then on ships, trains, automobiles, or airplanes. And, of course, there was the famous courier, Pheidippides, who carried the news of an Athenian victory over the Persians from the battlefield at Marathon to Athens in the 5th century BCE. More recently we had the organization of horseback couriers, the Pony Express, about which more follows on pp. 32–33.

## Animals, Boats, and Ships

Humans began to use animals to carry goods, messages, and the messengers who carried messages in their heads, something we still do. "You go tell Soandso that the price is $X, and that's final." Using animals to carry the messenger probably began about the same time as animals were domesticated, roughly 10,000 years ago. We also began to use inanimate objects—boats—to carry things. Probably the first of these craft were mere fallen trees floating in a stream; later came sailboats and paddleboats. Sailboats started as one- or two-person craft and grew to become ocean-crossing vessels. Paddleboats evolved into Roman triremes, shown in figure 2.3, propelled by banks of oarsmen—seaworthy but hardly something you'd want to be in when crossing the Atlantic in stormy weather.

Figure 2.3. *A Roman trireme.* Although these may have had a sail, the primary motive power came from the several banks of large oars. The power behind the oars tended to come from slaves. The use of oars gave extra speed and prevented the ship from being becalmed by lack of wind.

Probably the earliest use of animals for communication was in the Middle East, where people had camels, horses, and donkeys. They also had goats and sheep, but they are not much use as pack animals. Dogs were sometimes used as such in the Americas. As a means of communication, the larger animals could carry a person who carried a message, perhaps clay tablets or scrolls, and, of course, food for the trip and goods for trade. These animals extended the range of carrying goods and messages and increased the speed of travel compared to humans on foot. In my first and only camel ride, we went at about the pace of a person walking, not too fast. Our guides told us this was the usual rate. But, with the camel to carry messages, goods, food, and shelter, a group of people could cover more miles per day than if they had to bear their own loads.

Later horses, donkeys, and mules (an offspring of a horse and a donkey) could be hitched up to a wagon to carry even larger loads. This, of course, required roads, which we now see as channels of communication. Pigeons have been used to carry messages written on a small piece of paper or on small bits of photographic film attached to the bird's leg. In American history, the Pony Express was probably the most famous and romantic use of animals for communication. It was established in 1861 to carry mail from St. Joseph, Missouri, to Sacramento, California. It operated by having a series of outposts, each with fresh horses and sometimes fresh riders. As one rider drew in, he and his saddle bags changed horses and continued on to the next outpost. It took about a week to cover the full distance of the route.

Aquatic mammals, such as whales and dolphins, can communicate among themselves by sound. Dogs signal to each other and to their keepers by barking, and cats do it by meowing. In both cases the sounds vary depending upon what the animal wants to tell. Humans who live with animals soon learn to interpret the sounds, just as the pets learn the meaning of such sounds as *sit* or *come*. Songbirds produce sounds that may vary by type of bird and the nature of the message. Being birdbrained, birds don't send very complex messages, but they do want to attract a mate or warn their flock of danger; these messages must be distinct from all other bird calls if they are to be understood.

As we said, the first boats were probably tree trunks or branches that had fallen into water. A person could sit astride it and paddle with a flat piece of wood or push against the bottom with a pole. Gradually, people learned to hollow out a tree trunk by burning the center and scraping off the charred portions. Eventually, they made lighter and more easily controlled craft by assembling them out of flexible branches with thin coverings such as birch bark. These would be canoe-like boats. Next came sails. Like the use of animals to carry a load, adding a sail to a boat probably did not immediately increase speed so much as it decreased the work of the crew and, hence, the number of crew members needed to make a trip, which enabled people to take longer trips. Over the years, boats got better in strength and design—sails got bigger, steering mechanisms better—and one day we had the full-blown sailing ships in which Columbus and his crew could cross the Atlantic Ocean and explorers from many European countries could traverse the globe.

The ability of ships to travel so far depended on the design of hulls, sails, and rudders, as well as on navigation instruments that could tell the crew where a ship was and in what direction it was headed. The principal instruments were the magnetic compass that gave direction; the sextant, a device for measuring the angle above the horizon of heavenly bodies—stars or the sun—and a reliable clock that could keep good time in all the pitching of a small ship in high waves. The clock, combined with reading the angle of the sun above the horizon, could be used to tell how far east or west of a base line the ship was. The standard base line for longitude became the meridian that passes through Greenwich, England, where the British had established an astronomical observatory (see box opposite).

A sailing ship in the 15th through 17th centuries could take more than a month to cross the Atlantic, depending on wind, storms, and ocean currents. Later, when ships were steam powered, they no longer depended on favorable winds to make a trip. Gradually, they not only were free of worry about winds but increased their speed so that in 1952 the Atlantic could be crossed by the *S.S. United States* in as little as three and a half days, the fastest time ever recorded by an ocean liner.

But the sailing ships were enough to enable people to travel the world to trade and spread culture. While Europeans tended to impose aspects of their culture on other peoples, they also learned and brought back new ideas and new understanding of other peoples—communication.

## Iron Horses and Horseless Carriages

The steam engine (see box on p. 36 and figure 2.4 on p. 37) was invented in the 18th century and was first used for such jobs as pumping water out of mines, which did not require the engine to be able to move across the ground. As the engines got better and could be made smaller, they were installed on ships. Then a new engine on wheels, running on steel rails, pulling several carriages carrying freight or passengers behind it. The rails were smoother than dirt roads—no big bumps—and offered less resistance due to rails than along a dirt road. These locomotives were called "iron horses."

***Measuring latitude and longitude.*** Noon, anywhere on earth, is when the sun is at its highest point for the day. It may not be directly overhead, but its angle with the horizon will be no higher than at noon. A book of astronomical tables can tell, given the date, at what latitude you must be once you have this height measurement. To make the measurement you use an instrument called a *sextant*. Similar instruments were used by Arabian mariners as long ago as the 10th century. The sextant was invented in 1759.

*Latitude* tells how far above or below the equator you are. But, how far east or west of some established line are you? That measurement is called *longitude*. To measure it, first you need a fixed line from which to measure. The meridian passing through the British Royal Observatory at Greenwich, England, was accepted as a standard by most countries in 1884. A meridian is one of the imaginary lines running north and south through the North and South Poles. The Greenwich meridian is called the Prime Meridian, the line from which measurements are made. The time there used to be called Greenwich Mean Time but is now called Universal Coordinated Time. If you know the time where you are and you have some way to know the time in Greenwich, you would know how long it has taken the sun to travel to where you are. (Of course the sun doesn't travel, but it seems to.) If it is 6 P.M. where you are and noon in Greenwich, you are six sun hours away and, again using a table, you can find out your longitude.

This sounds pretty easy, but making a clock that could keep good time given the motion of a ship and the changing temperatures placed great demands on clock making. This, of course, was before electric clocks or time signals over the radio or Internet. An adequate ship's clock was invented in 1759, although it took several years for its inventor, John Harrison, to receive full recognition for his work. It made sea travel much safer.

Today we use the Global Positioning System (GPS) that delivers accurate positions from an artificial satellite to a receiver by radio. See chapter 4.

The first steam railway trains were built in 1802 in England, 1805 in the United States. Within about 50 years both countries had tracks criss-crossing the land. Railroads carried passengers and freight, and freight included mail. Around the time of the American Revolution mail service was not like it is now. Service between was haphazard at best and there was no real service to the west. The west then could have meant areas around present-day Pittsburgh or Buffalo or the really far west—Ohio. Sending mail to these places depended on finding a traveler who might be going to somewhere near the destination of the letter and who might be willing to carry it. But 19th-century trains went to many cities. At the height of their use in the 1940s and 1950s, steam trains could cross the country in three to four days. Railroads improved the speed, carrying capacity, safety of travel, and much more. Henry David Thoreau asked, "Have not men improved in punctuality

---

*Steam engines* work by first heating water to the boiling point to generate steam, which is a much-expanded form of water. Having expanded, the steam pushes hard against the containing boiler. The boiler is heated by a fire. In the 19th century on trains or ships the fire would have been fueled by wood or coal; in the 20th often by oil.

Once the steam is generated, it passes through a pipe to a piston, which is connected to a wheel. Steam pushes against the piston, pushing it along a cylinder. That force causes the wheel to turn. As the piston moves, as in figure 2.4, some of the energy of the original push goes to moving the piston back to its original position, ready for more steam. Notice that the boiler, where the fire burns or combustion takes place, was separated from the piston the steam is driving.

Steam engines did a better job of propelling ships than sails did, and of pulling trains than wind, horses, or mules could. But they were somewhat cumbersome. They tended to be large and demanded a great deal of fuel. The biggest car on an early railroad train was the locomotive or engine; a second car was needed to hold its supply of coal or wood. Also, a steam engine is not highly efficient in the sense of how much energy of the fuel can be converted into mechanical energy. It is not surprising, therefore, that engineers began looking for something smaller that used less fuel.

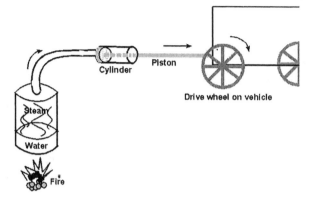

Figure 2.4. *Elements of a steam engine.* The steam is created in
a boiler containing water and then piped to a cylinder where the
power of the expanding steam drives a piston, which, in turn,
drives a wheel. The boiler and the piston can be quite distant
from each other, possibly aboard the vehicle being powered or on
the ground near a pump, mill, or other stationary machinery.

since the railroad was invented? Do they not talk and think faster
in the depot than they did in the stage-office? . . . To do things
'railroad fashion' is now the by-word."[6]

By the start of the 20th century roads had improved to the
point where a motorized vehicle might out-perform the horse and
wagon. These vehicles were propelled by internal combustion
engines described in the box and figure 2.5 on p. 38. The result
was the automobile, first created in Germany in 1885 by Gottlieb
Daimler (see figure 2.6). Motor-driven cars and trucks eventually
became so popular that we now seem somewhat inundated by
them. They are the means by which individuals and packages are
delivered right to your door. These, of course, were the "horseless
carriages."

*Internal combustion engines*, like their steam cousins, use hot gases to push a piston, which then drives a wheel or propeller. But now, the fire is *inside* the cylinder that holds the piston; hence, the combustion is internal. In a gasoline or natural gas engine, some fuel is sprayed into the cylinder and mixed with air. The piston then moves to compress this mixture and a spark is fired into the cylinder. There is then an explosion, although it is controlled. The combustion creates hot gases, which expand explosively, pushing the piston to the other end of the cylinder (see figure 2.5) and is then ready for a new cycle. A diesel engine does not use a spark. When it compresses the oil-gas mixture, so much heat is created that the mixture ignites without a spark. Internal combustion engines are, in general, more efficient than steam engines, much smaller, and need less fuel. You simply cannot run a modern airplane with a steam engine.

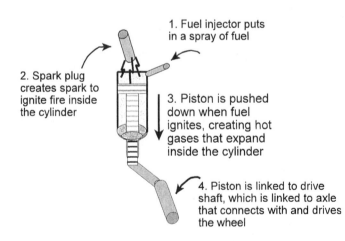

1. Fuel injector puts in a spray of fuel

2. Spark plug creates spark to ignite fire inside the cylinder

3. Piston is pushed down when fuel ignites, creating hot gases that expand inside the cylinder

4. Piston is linked to drive shaft, which is linked to axle that connects with and drives the wheel

Figure 2.5. *Elements of an internal combustion engine.* A piston is driven by expanding gases as in the steam engine, but this time the gas is created inside the cylinder by igniting a fuel-air mixture. Because the source of the power is within the cylinder, which is directly connected to a drive shaft, such an engine is more compact than a steam engine and is more efficient in its use of fuel.

Figure 2.6. *The first Daimler automobile.* Herr Daimler is in the rear seat. The car, built in 1886, looks much like a carriage to be drawn by a horse. Photo courtesy of DaimlerChrysler Classic Archives.

# Flying Machines

It took about 100 years to go from the first steam-driven vehicles—ships and trains—to vehicles driven by internal combustion engines. The idea that humans could fly is quite old, going back at least to the Greek myth of Icarus, who devised a set of wax wings and could fly by using them. Unfortunately, so the story goes, he flew too close to the sun, his wings melted, and that was the end of Icarus.[7]

In reality, flight began with hot air balloons, a form of which are still in use, mainly for sport. The first ones were built in France in 1783. Their main practical use was as observation platforms in war. A limitation was that balloons like these could not be steered. They simply went where the wind took them, unless anchored to the ground by a long rope. It was another century before someone put a motor into a balloon and created the steerable airship, the latest version of which is held aloft by a bag of helium gas instead of hot air and which we now see at sports events as the Goodyear blimp.

Around 1900, Orville and Wilbur Wright, brothers from Dayton, Ohio, conceived of a motor-driven vehicle that could fly using wings for lift rather than a large gas or hot air balloon. The motor drove a propeller that pushed the airplane. Theirs pushed; most now pull. Wind under the wings provided the lift somewhat the same as wind raises a kite. Very roughly, the faster the plane moved, the more lift it got and the higher the plane could fly. The first flight was at Kitty Hawk, North Carolina, on December 17, 1903.

When World War I began in 1914, planes had progressed so far that they were used for reconnaissance like the old ball-oons—flying over the enemy to see what was going on. Quickly, other planes were developed to shoot at the reconnaissance planes and also to drop bombs on the ground. Blimp-like airships were able to go from Germany to England to drop bombs. Figure 2.7 shows the progression of aircraft from the first Wright Brothers' plane (1903) to the Concorde, the world's fastest airliner.

Peaceful uses of aviation were also developing. In 1914 we had the first passenger-carrying air service that flew only across Tampa Bay, but it was a start. In 1918 the first air mail service in the United States was introduced. In 1920, the service carried forty-nine million letters. In 1919 some U.S. Navy planes crossed the Atlantic but with a stopover at an island along the way. In 1927 Charles A. Lindbergh flew alone nonstop from New York to Paris and was acclaimed a great hero. Today, air travelers can go almost anywhere in the world and air mail is the primary means of moving mail over long distances. The British Airways–Air France Concorde could cross the Atlantic in about three hours, at its top speed of 2179 kilometers per hour, but these planes were expensive to operate and their commercial use was discontinued in 2003.

––––––––––

The only means of long-distance communication by primitive peoples were drums and other sound-making instruments, light from the sun enabling one person to be seen by another from hundreds of meters away, and light used for signaling. These early people could also carry messages or make use of an animal or boat to carry the messenger. Before steam-driven ships and trains (early

Figure 2.7. *Development of the airplane.* Here we see (top left) the original Wright Brothers flyer; (top right) a World War I Sopwith Camel, a favorite with pilots of the age and of Snoopy, the modern cartoon dog; (bottom left) the Douglas DC-3, brought out in the 1930s and for some twenty years the work horse of commercial aviation; and (bottom right) the Anglo-French supersonic airliner, Concorde, the fastest airliner ever built. The Concorde could go from Paris to New York in about three hours, but eventually proved uneconomical to operate.

1800s) ground or sea modes of communication had not changed dramatically since ancient times. The biggest change before steam ships was in navigation instruments that made it safe for sailing ships to venture far into the oceans.

With the steam engine and later the internal combustion engine, the speed and carrying capacity of land-, sea-, and air-based vehicles improved enormously so that travel across an ocean or continent has become a matter of hours not months. They improved mail service and the movement of people who thereby became able to observe other cultures and meet new people. These forms of communication set in motion the radical change of the old world into our modern world.

# Notes

1. Polo, *The Travels*.
2. Clarke, *How the World Was Won*, p. 3.
3. Nevins and Commager, *A Short History of the United States*, p. 124.
4. Carrington, *Talking Drums of Africa*.
5. McLuhan, *Understanding Media*, p. 8.
6. Thoreau, *Walden*, pp. 134–36.
7. Hamilton, Mythology,. pp. 139–40.

# Further Reading

## General

Singer. et al. *A History of Technology*. This eight-volume work, published in the 1950s, has an article on just about any technology invented before then. Not available in all libraries, but quite a find if it is.

## East–West Travel—The Silk Road

Elisseeff. *The Silk Roads: Highways of Culture and Commerce*.
"History of the Silk Road" (Web site).

## Early Steam and Land Transport Vehicles

Briggs. *The Power of Steam*.
Chandler. *The Railroads*.
Cole. "Land Transport without Wheels."
Marsden. *Watt's Perfect Engine*.
McShane. *The Automobile*.
Robbins. *The Railway Age*.

## Boats and Ships

Angelucci and Cucari. *Ship*.
Landstrom. *The Ship*.

## Navigation

Aczel. *The Riddle of the Compass*.
Bennett. *The Divided Circle*.
Finamore. *Maritime History as World History*.
Heyerdahl. *Early Man and the Ocean*.
Johansen. "History of Navigation."
"Navigational Instruments" (Web site).
Randier. *Marine Navigation Instruments*.
Sobel. *Longitude*.
Tooley. *Maps and Map-Makers*.

## Animal Transportation—Pony Express

Bradley. *The Story of the Pony Express*.
Cullinan. *The United States Postal Service*.
Oslin. *The Story of Telecommunications*.

## Sound Waves and Their Use

Berg and Stork. *The Physics of Sound*.
Knight. *The First Book of Sound*.

## Flying Machines

*Century of Flight* / by the Editors of Time-Life Books.
Smithsonian Institution. *Milestones of Aviation*.

# 3

# History of Communication: Photography and Electricity

In the 19th century science and technology began to move ahead rapidly. The steam engine, originally invented in the 18th century, improved so that it could be installed in a ship or railway carriage, which enabled transportation to gain in speed, range of travel, and load carried. Electricity was known but not put to much practical use until the mid-19th century, which is when technology became so important in culture and commerce. Photography did not depend on a power source but on chemistry before it could become a frequently used and depended-upon medium. At just about the same time that photography became practical and widespread in use, the electric telegraph also became practical, first in England and then in an improved form in the United States. The telephone came soon after.

# Photography

Photography is a means of recording a visual image onto a surface such as a sheet of paper. Of course, people had been drawing for thousands of years, but the goal of photography was to make a true copy of what the eye could see. Today, most of us recognize that the camera's lens sees somewhat differently than does the eye of the observer. For example, while a good camera or the human eye can see a beautiful array of colors, dogs cannot see much color. Some cameras can see infrared light, which humans cannot.

As with other inventions, there were early experiments that came to very little, some going as far back as the year 750 CE. In 1822, in France, Joseph Niépce worked out a way to record an image on a stone or sheet of metal. He was a lithographer. Lithography is a technique for recording an image in ink on a flat stone, then transferring it to paper. (*Litho* is from a Greek word meaning stone.) His method worked well, but it took eight hours to make the image using the light of the sun.

In 1839, again in France, Louis Daguerre invented the *daguerreotype*. He used a copper plate coated with silver iodide, which turns black when exposed to light but retains its original light color if not exposed. This gave a negative image, but if the picture is held at an appropriate angle to the light, the values reverse and appear positive. You can sometimes see this effect with black print on a glossy white surface, such as a magazine page. If you hold the paper at an angle so that the ink, which may be shiny even if black, reflects the light source directly toward your eye, it seems lighter than the paper does. Daguerre's invention became very popular. Examples can still be seen in many museums. Ten years later in 1849 Frederick Archer of England began using glass plates covered with different chemicals. His method produced a negative image, but the use of glass plates made it easy to take a picture of the negative picture that would now be a "positive," or one that shows light-colored objects as white and dark ones as black (see box opposite and figure 3.1 on p. 48).

*Negative and Positive Images in Photography.* Modern photographic film consists of a transparent plastic sheet on top of which is a layer of a chemical, usually silver bromide. This chemical reacts to light. If you looked at the film immediately after it had been exposed to light, you would see no effect, but if you immerse the film in another chemical, *developing fluid,* the exposed areas of the silver bromide on the film turn black. Unexposed areas remain transparent. The more light in a portion of the image, the darker the corresponding portion of the film turns. You can get black or white areas or many shades of grey in between. What you get, then, is a picture in which dark areas of the original scene are light, and light originals are dark. That hardly wins prizes in photo contests. What you have to do is reverse this. How? Take a picture of the picture, get a negative of the negative and original light areas are now light, dark areas are dark. The second picture is made in the dark room, using an enlarger, rather than the original camera, but it functions as a camera. See figure 3.1.

There are photo chemicals that make *direct positives*, skipping the negative phase. In spite of the extra step, the two-step process works better in most cases.

In 1889 in the United States, Thomas Edison invented a way of projecting a series of photographs of a moving subject, each image being slightly different from the preceding one, which makes the result look like the images were moving. And so, the movies were born. Two French brothers, Auguste and Louis Lumière, having seen Edison's work, went home and improved on his invention.

Early still cameras used glass plates covered with a chemical emulsion containing the light-sensitive material. The cameras were large and heavy by today's standards. In 1888, George Eastman, founder of the Eastman Kodak Co., began using paper coated with this emulsion. The new film could easily be wrapped around a spool and enabled the use of small, highly portable box cameras (named for the shape). A year later, he introduced a nitrocellulose film as the base for the emulsion. This flexible, transparent plastic material is essentially what we still use today in film cameras, which are now being largely replaced by digital cameras. East-man's early box cameras eventually became today's 35 millimeter cameras and these, in turn, are fast being replaced by the latest invention, the digital camera, which does not use film. These newest cameras record an image on a tiny chip, which must be read into a computer or printer and reconstituted as a visual image.

Photography quickly became a means of recording news, family events, illustrations for books, copies of legal documents, and movies. Photographs are an art form in themselves, not just because of the images they copy. Perhaps more than any other invention until television, photography reminds us of the importance of communicating by means of images rather than only by words.

Figure 3.1. *Processing negative images in photography*. The image of two light grey rabbits, left, is what the subject looked like to the eye, except that here it is black and white. The middle image is what the first image looks like when a negative photo is made of it. Original dark spots are light and light spots are dark. When a second picture, right, is taken of the negative image the result is a positive, just like the original. Photo by the author.

## The Telegraph

During Queen Victoria's reign (1837 to 1901), electricity sparked interest in being used as a means of sending messages. All the early forms involved sending a pulse of electric current along a wire that would light a lamp or move some object at the receiving end. That action served as a symbol. For example, the current could cause a pointer to indicate a letter, or create a sound by causing one piece of metal to strike another, or light up a lamp for different periods of time, or briefly sound a buzzer. The enormous advantage of this form of transmission is that it could send a signal over very long distances virtually instantaneously.

Remember that the Pony Express in the American West could carry a message by horseback from St. Joseph, Missouri, to Sacramento, California, in about a week. The telegraph, by doing the job in seconds, put this romantic form of communication out of business. Well, perhaps it was minutes if the message had to be received and re-transmitted along the way. There was almost nothing in human history comparable to this ratio: a week to, say, a minute—a ratio of some 10,000 to 1 in transmission time. Telegraphs were invented in many places, but good working models by Charles Wheatstone and William Cooke (see figure 3.2 on p. 50) were first used in England in 1837 by the Great Western Railway and later in 1844 in the United States by Samuel F. B. Morse.

Morse had been an artist who on a visit to England became fascinated with the idea of an electric telegraph. On returning home, he assembled a team that produced a working, efficient telegraph system, which he was able to demonstrate to Congress in 1844 by sending his famous message, "What hath God wrought" from Baltimore to Washington. At first many independent telegraph companies were formed, most of which were soon amalgamated into the Western Union Telegraph Company. This company's name is still in use, although now the service is primarily for transferring money. A message goes from the originator at one location to tell a receiving Western Union office how much to give to whom. Just about all other telegraph functions have now been taken over by fax, electronic mail, or file transfers that allow us to send and receive in the home or office and require no encoding or decoding by humans.

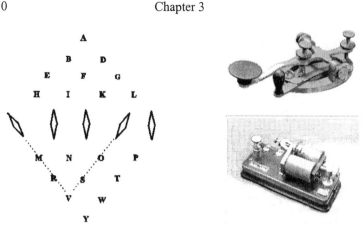

Figure 3.2. *Early telegraph instruments.* The image at left shows the display of the receiving apparatus of the Cooke-Wheatstone telegraph that was in use in 1837, before Morse patented his much simpler devices. The letter sent is the only one pointed to by two of the "needles." In this case it is the letter V. Note that there is no J, C, Q, U, X, or Z. An example of a Morse-style transmitter is at right top, and a receiver at right bottom. The Morse transmitter, or key, is simply a switch to complete or break a circuit. The receiver has an electromagnet that pulls one piece of metal against another, making a sound. Other receivers could record a pen mark showing a short or long interval of closed circuit, or sound a buzzer. The Morse instruments are courtesy of the American Museum of Radio and Electricity.

The telegraph was, well, electrifying in its effect. There was a drawback, though. People did not tend to have telegraph keys in their homes or offices, and each sender and receiver had to be directly linked by wire. Messages had to be taken to a central office to be keyed and sent to the destination. So, to send a message meant first going to the telegraph office; receiving a message meant that a messenger had to travel from the telegraph office to the home or office of the intended recipient. These trips took time; they brought us back to the days of carrying messages all the way, but the two telegraph offices involved could be hundreds, even thousands of miles apart. Of course, we also had to erect poles and string wires from one to another, over mountains and across rivers (see figure 3.3). Finally, the telegraph could not carry the human voice. It carried the equivalent of text—a message was written, converted into code (Morse code), transmitted, then reconverted to human-readable text. Still, the gain in total transmission time over the use of messengers was enormous.

Figure 3.3. *Stringing early telegraph wires.* Bringing the telegraph into the expanding West was difficult work. Workers had to span rivers and cross mountains. The wires often followed the railroad since the railroads were major customers and could, of course, carry the men and supplies needed directly to the work site. Photo courtesy of Union Pacific Historical Collection.

As an example of the pretelegraph difficulty of comumun-ication, consider a business person in the American West of the early 19th century. A place like Nashville was considered to be in the far west. A shopkeeper wanting to buy supplies might have to get them from Philadelphia, both a center of manu-facturing and an import-ant commercial seaport. But, the buyer could not know the price that would be charged when the order was received, which might be many days after it was sent. Similarly, a farmer from around Nashville could ship produce to market in New Orleans by ship, but again, the delay in transport meant he could not know the price he would receive when the goods arrived.[1]

An indication of the importance of the telegraph, especially to business, was the laying of the Atlantic cable, a telegraph cable that stretched from Newfoundland to Ireland. Much of this was sponsored by Cyrus Field, an American businessman, but it re-quired the cooperation of other companies and the United States and British governments. The end points were chosen because they gave the shortest distance across the Atlantic Ocean. Communica-tion from the end points to the major centers of the United States and Britain was much less of a problem because transmission was over conventional telegraph wires on land or the short span of water between Ireland and England.

## The Telephone

Remember two important things about the telegraph: (1) It cannot transmit voices or music, only messages that can be encoded by breaks of varying length in an electric current. The sound, if the circuit contains a buzzer or bell, would go on and off as the circuit is closed and broken. The sound is always the same; what varies is the duration of a "dot" or "dash," and (2) the operator of a tele-graph needs quite a bit of skill. He or she must learn Morse code. But just as a musician cannot merely learn what the musical symbols mean on a score, but must be able to play them well, the telegraph operator must be able to send code using the right length of time for dots, dashes, and the space between letters and words. All this must be consistent. There is a rhythm to it. As a matter of fact, just as an expert violinist can recognize the style of another expert, an expert telegrapher can recognize what they called the "fist" of another operator.

Alexander Graham Bell was born in Scotland, moved to Canada, and then to the United States. While in Canada he became interested in developing a machine that could carry the human voice over wires (see box below). Canadians believe he invented the telephone in Canada, but all agree that it was when we was in Boston, Massachusetts, in 1876, that he first got it to work. He then registered with the Patent Office shortly before his first actual

---

*Transmitting voices by electricity.* Humans do not speak or make vocal sounds of a single frequency. If you pluck a guitar string or strike a tuning fork, you get a *pure tone*—sound of a single frequency although the guitar's sound box may add some additional frequencies. How do we get all this information into a single current to be sent out as a telephone message? First, the telephone system does not transmit sound. Sound is converted to electricity in your telephone instrument and electricity is converted back to sound in the recipient's telephone. Everything in between is electric current.

Inside the speaker or transmitter part of the phone is a diaphragm, a thin metal plate that vibrates like a drum head as we speak. Under the diaphragm is a box of charcoal granules that when compressed by the diaphragm's vibrations create a low-voltage electric current. This current varies with the frequency of the vibrations. The variation in the current is then quite complex, unlike a series of waves all the same height and length. It is not just a matter of current or no current. The initially weak current has to be amplified along the way. At the receiver, it goes through an electromagnet, which in turn pulls on a diaphragm to make it vibrate the same way the one in the transmitter did. And so, we have a voice message sent and received. Early telephones did not reproduce the voice exactly, but you could hear the words clearly and usually recognize a friend's voice. Today, we get much better reception.

success. Interestingly, another man, Elisha Gray, filed for a similar invention on the *same day*. But at the Patent Office it's who gets there first that matters, and Bell beat Gray by a matter of hours. Amos E. Dolbear filed a claim in the same year.[2] Still another claim was recently made on behalf of Antonio Meucci, a new immigrant to the United States from Italy, who was said to have produced a working model of a telephone in 1860, but was without funds and did not know how to protect his invention.[3] A German scientist, Philipp Reis, is said to have invented the phone as early as 1861.[4] None of these claims reduce the accomplishments of Bell, who made the telephone a household instrument. Some telephones dating from 1876 to 2004 are shown in figure 3.4.

Bell's timing was magnificent in another way, too. The world seemed to be waiting for just this machine. A phone could be put in the home, in the store, or in the office. No codes were needed. Almost anyone could operate it. At first, every phone had to be linked by wire to any other phone to which the owner might want to talk. This, of course, could mean a great deal of wire if the newfangled thing were really popular. Within two years of the basic invention, central switching stations were invented. These were linked to each telephone subscriber in an area, but each telephone needed to be linked only to the central station. From there, a call could be connected to an outgoing wire leading to any other telephone that was connected to the same office. This saved much wire and expense.

Soon someone got the idea that central offices could be linked to each other, perhaps only by a single wire cable. Then a caller in one city could reach a phone in another city by having the call connected through a series of central offices as shown in figure 3.5 on p. 56. That is how long-distance telephoning is done.

To make a call, a user picked up the handset of the phone and turned a crank (see right side of image in figure 3.4b and c) which caused a circuit between this phone and the central office to be closed, which, in turn, lit a light or sounded a bell at central. An *operator* would connect to the caller and ask, "Number please." The caller gave the number of the phone to be reached and an electrical link was then established between caller and destination.

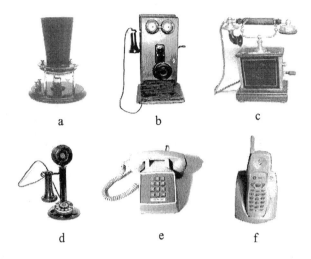

Figure 3.4. *Development of the telephone.* Here are six wired telephones, spanning the period 1876 to 2000. A replica of Bell's first telephone of 1876, with a single instrument serving for both speaking and receiving is at a. A Canadian phone that served a typical home of about the 1890s is at b. A more elegant phone from Denmark, produced between 1907 and 1920 is at c. An early American dial telephone from the 1920s is at d, a typical early push-button phone from about 1970 at e, and a modern remote phone from about 2000 at f. The remote part of this phone is a radio; the base part is a wired telephone plus a radio receiver. Photo credits: a and d American Museum of Radio and Electricity, b Collection of Ian and Linda Samuels, c and e collection of the author, f collection of Stephen Goring.

Eventually, there got to be so many telephones in use that this process had to be automated. In 1891 a *rotary dial* telephone was invented similar to that shown in figure 3.4d. These were not really common until the 1930s. In order to dial a number, say 3456 (four digits were enough in the early days), you put a finger in the hole corresponding to the digit wanted and rotated the dial until the finger hit a stopping device, then let it go. See the dial close-up in

figure 3.6. A spring would then begin to return the dial to its
original position. As it went back, the phone emitted a clicking
sound for each hole that got to or beyond the stopping device. In
this case, it would first emit three clicks, then another finger action
followed by four clicks, then five, then six, and then the action
would stop. A primitive computer at central now knew you wanted
to dial telephone number 3456. Push-button, or Touch Tone®,
phones were put into use around 1963. With these, as a button is
pushed a coded signal is sent to the switching center. This is now
the main way to "dial" a number.

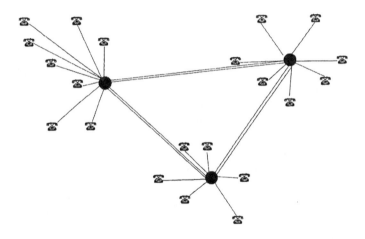

Figure 3.5. *The role of a central switching office.* Without a
"central," it was necessary to have a line from each telephone to
each other phone the owner wanted to be able to reach. Even in
the early days of telephoning, this was a significant burden. The
central switch meant that each phone need only be connected to
one central office, which could switch an incoming call to the
line to the destination's telephone. Later, central offices in distant
cities were connected, shown here by double lines, giving subscribers long-distance service.

Figure 3.6. *Rotary dial for a telephone.* The user inserts a finger into the hole corresponding to the desired digit or letter. A number has three letters with it, so that the third hole can stand for 3, D, E, or F. Then the dial is rotated clockwise until the finger hits the stop at about 3 o'clock. On withdrawing the finger, the dial springs back to its starting position, transmitting clicks as it goes. Three clicks = the number 3.

The growth of the telephone industry was amazing. Bell's first company became the Bell Telephone Company. A variety of mergers and split-offs resulted in creation of the American Telephone & Telegraph Company (AT&T) in 1885. AT&T was initially a subsidiary, but for reasons of laws governing the sale of shares, AT&T became the parent corporation. In 2005 Cingular, a mobile telephone company, moved to take over AT&T. Whether the name will survive remains uncertain as this is written.

Figure 3.7 shows the number of phone lines installed in the United States from 1876 to 2000. And it is still growing. One change that supported growth was combining telephone with radio. Radio was originally used to send messages across oceans or from ship to shore. In the 1950s, it was sometimes used instead of wire, especially when it was necessary to cross a river or mountain ridge. Following this came the mobile telephone—a radio in an auto where the radio was linked to a telephone switching center. The big jump came with the cellular telephone (see figure 3.8). Again, the cell phone is actually a radio, but the new method allowed for far more telephones to be used as portables. Today, cell phones are being called Personal Communication Systems (PCS) or mobile telephones (see chapter 4) and they can not only carry voice messages, but handle e-mail and other computer functions and can even take and transmit pictures. The multiple use of a single technology is an example of *convergence*, about which we'll have more to say in chapter 12.

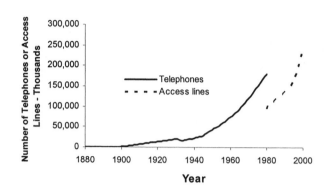

Figure 3.7. *Growth of the telephone industry in the United States.* This graph shows the number of installed phone lines in the United States from 1880 to 2000. In 1980 such statistics began to be based on access lines instead of installed phones because of the proliferation of extensions and local switchboards, giving many phones for a single line. These figures do not include cell phones, which do not use lines.[4]

Figure 3.8. *A modern wireless telephone.* This is a Treo 600 manufactured by PalmOne, Inc. The design of this type of phone and the functions it can perform change rapidly as it approaches being not just a voice transmitter and receiver, but a computer and camera that communicates. Photo courtesy PalmOne, Inc.

Cell phones or wireless phones have proven beneficial in places where there had not previously been wire-based telephones. Such places included developing countries—countries whose economic situation did not permit the building and widespread use of wire-based telephone systems. They also include remote parts of large, developed countries such as the United States and Canada. Cell phone instruments cost more than wire telephones, but there is no cost for stringing and maintaining wire.

---

In this chapter we described the beginnings of the new science and technology of communication. First, there was chemistry that gave us the new medium of photography as a way to record pictorial images. Then came the use of electricity in two important inventions: the telegraph and the telephone. The telegraph was capable only of sending coded messages, but it was so much faster than anything that had come before it that it made a huge change in the way business and government were conducted. For example, in 1864 General Sherman gave the telegraph a large share of the credit for his successful (as the Union forces saw it) foray into Georgia in the American Civil War. The telephone brought us the ability to send our voices over a wire—to speak in plain language, not encoding the messages. Because it was so easy to use, it was quickly found in homes and offices. Today, nearly every home in North America has a telephone. Many countries that had not had well-developed phone systems that depended on wire for transmission skipped right over the wire form of telephoning to cell phones.

The world was now getting used to major changes in communication. Could the telephone or something like it be extended to cross oceans? We'll see in chapter 4.

## Notes

1. Nevins and Commager, *A Short History of the United States*, p. 191.
2. Brooks. *Telephone*, pp. 74–78.
3. *Historical Statistics of the United States* and *Statistical Abstracts of the United States*.
4. Katz, "Johann Philipp Reis" (Web site).
5. U.S. Congress. House. HR 269. 107th Congress.

# Further Reading

## Photography

Bridges. "Oldest Known Photograph."
"Directory of Notable Photographers" (Web site).
Hirsch. *Seizing the Light.*
Langford. *The Story of Photography from Its Beginnings to the Present Day.*

## Telegraph

Coe. *The Telegraph.*
Oslin. *The Story of Telecommunications.*
Sherman. *Memoirs of General William T. Sherman*, pp. 888–91.
Silverman. *Lightning Man.*
Standage. *The Victorian Internet.*

## Atlantic Cable

Carter. *Cyrus Field.*
Clarke. *How the World Was Won*, pp. 17–27.
Oslin. *The Story of Telecommunications*, pp. 157–86.

## Telephone

Brooks. *Telephone, the First Hundred Years.*
Caldwell. "Atlanta Telephone History" (Web site).
Casson. "Who Really Invented the Telephone?" (Web site).
Catania. "Antonio Meucci Revisited" (Web site).
Coe. *The Telephone and Its Several Inventors.*
Grosvenor and Wesson. *Alexander Graham Bell.*
Oslin. *The Story of Telecommunications*, pp. 213–34.
Pool. *The Social Impact of the Telephone.*
U.S. Congress. House. HR 269. 107th Cong. (Concerns the Meucci claim.)

# 4

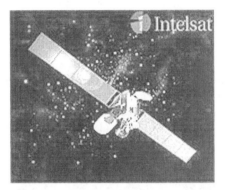

# History of Communication: Electronics

For any of the electronic technologies described in this chapter, it is difficult to pick one person and say that he or she is the sole inventor. Too many people had a hand in it or worked independently at the same time as the person usually named as inventor. In this book, I try to name the main people responsible for the ideas and the ones responsible for bringing the ideas into practical reality—not just getting an idea for radio, for example, but for making it a widely useful and available device. Similar fogginess exists with regard to dates. Many inventions evolved rather slowly over several years, leaving exact dates for crediting any given invention rather vague.

# Radio

The essence of radio is that electromagnetic waves (see box below) travel through space and can be detected by an electrical conductor such as a wire or metal pole. There were three theoretical scientists most responsible for the ideas underlying radio, the harnessing of electromagnetic waves to carry information.

*Electromagnetic waves* are energy waves. They can be created on earth and sent to anywhere on earth or other bodies in space. Their intensity can be varied. If done correctly the variations can carry information, just as varying an electric current could transmit messages in the telegraph or telephone. Radio waves are one form of electromagnetic waves. So are light, medical X-rays, and cosmic rays.

Michael Faraday was British and lived from 1791 to 1867. He noticed that if a magnetic field moved, an electric current was created in a wire within the field. This is called *induction*. A *field*, in physics, is a space in which some force is active, acting on everything within the space. A magnet creates such a field around itself. If you move an electrical conductor through the magnetic field, a current is set up in the conductor. It may be very slight, but it's there.

James Clerk Maxwell, also British, lived from 1831 to 1879. He recognized that induction works the other way, too. Not only would a magnetic field induce a current in a wire or conductor in a magnetic field, but a current in an electrical conductor creates a magnetic field around itself. Maxwell's principal accomplishment was to give a mathematical description of electromagnetic waves. He was primarily a scientist and did not work on applications of his discoveries.

Figure 4.1 shows electromagnetic waves moving and imping-ing on a metal antenna, an electrical conductor. The set up a cur-

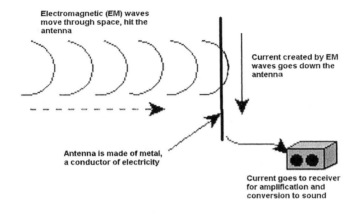

Figure 4.1. *The concept of electrical induction.* Michael Faraday's discovery in 1831 is what produces an electric current in a radio antenna when electromagnetic waves pass through it. The current is weak but can be amplified to give good quality radio and television reception.

rent in the antenna. This current flows into the receiver, where it is amplified and converted to sound.

Is the magnetic field actually "in the air"? Not exactly. The field can be created without air, in a vacuum. Air is not necessary to carry radio signals, but in the early days people could not conceive of waves moving through nothing, so some assumed the air was a carrier, some a substance called *ether*, which was found not to exist. (This was different from the ether used as an anaesthetic.) We pick up radio waves from distant stars—with no air between us and them.

Heinrich Hertz (1857-1894), in Germany, was probably the first person to use Maxwell's findings to produce radio waves in the laboratory and measure their properties. He, too, was a scientist, not an inventor, and did not go on to make any practical machines from his discoveries. However, he may have been the true inventor of radio.

In the 1890s an Italian, Guglielmo Marconi (1874–1937), more an inventor than a research scientist, began to experiment with radio waves on his own. In his first try he transmitted across a room, then over 1,700 meters, and soon across the English Channel from France to England (56 kilometers or about 33 miles). By 1901 he had set up a famous experiment to see if he could transmit a signal from Cornwall in England to Newfoundland (now part of Canada). It worked. This is a distance of about 3,500 kilometers, or 2,170 miles. By 1896 he had a patent on some of his radio equipment and by 1904 he had his radio installed in 124 ships at sea. It was attractive for ships because you could not, after all, string wires between ships and the shore or between two ships at sea. Radio gave them the ability to communicate over very long distances.

What Marconi had was *wireless telegraphy*. He could send Morse code signals but not his voice. Just as with the telephone his radio was only capable of sending out electromagnetic waves at a single frequency and turning them on and off. Converted to sound, these variations became "dots" and "dashes." Those ships that used his "wireless," as the new invention was called, needed a professional radio operator, just as the telegraph did. Shortly before the *Titanic* hit an iceberg in 1912, it picked up radio signals from another ship, the *Californian*, warning about ice in the area near Newfoundland, toward which the *Titanic* was steaming. The warning was ignored. When the *Titanic* struck the iceberg and was sinking, it sent out distress signals by radio. These could have been picked up by the *Californian*, but its radio operator had gone off duty just before the distress signal was sent, so no one nearby heard it. *Californian* was near enough that it might have been able to save most of the passengers had its captain known enough of what was happening to make the try.

Even as wireless telegraphy, Marconi's radio was a success, used by commercial ships as well as armies and navies. To ships, it was a safety device. To passengers with urgent business, it was a means of keeping in touch with the family and the office.

The idea of sending voice and music by radio was a dream of many people. The basic problem was the need for more signaling capacity since more information was needed to encode the full frequency range of the human voice or of music (see box below). Notable among those who tried was the Canadian Reginald Fessenden. He was able to transmit a musical program in 1906. But he got no further at the time. It was one thing to send so complex a signal, another to build all the equipment needed to transmit and receive, create the broadcasting studios, and get receivers into the hands of enough users to make it all worthwhile.

A Marconi engineer named David Sarnoff foresaw the future of broadcast radio. He urged the American branch of Marconi's company to produce what he first called "radio music boxes," but World War I diverted attention from such a new enterprise. In 1918

---

*Signal capacity or bandwidth.* Radio and television use a series of electromagnetic waves to send information. How much information can be sent in, say, one second depends on the frequencies available to the transmitter. Suppose a sender could send only one wave per second. How much information can be put into that one wave? Not much, since both the speed and wave length are limited. Hence, all we can vary much is the amplitude or height or power of a wave. A small change might not be noticeable by a receiver and this limits the amount of information that can be sent by amplitude change alone. So, suppose we can only change its amplitude from high to low. That still allows the sending of a signal of the yes-no or dot-dash variety (low amplitude: dot, high: dash). But, one dot or dash per second can't bring you color television with surround sound.

A modern FM or TV transmitter needs millions of waves per second. Each broadcaster is allowed only a limited portion of the whole range of frequencies to be sure that signals do not interfere with each other. So, a radio or television broadcasting station is given a certain frequency range and its signals must stay within that range. (See Government Regulation box, p. 71.) For television, the range is 6 mHz (mHz = megahertz or 1 million hertz), the difference between the highest and lowest frequencies in the range. Each station is told which 6 mHz to use. That range is called the available *bandwidth*. Bandwidth to electronic media is like fuel for an airplane or food for a wolf. Without enough, they can't do the job they set out to do.

after the end of the war, the U.S. government realized the growing importance of radio, both for commercial and government purposes. They were unhappy about having something so important in the hands of a foreign-owned company (Marconi), so they worked out an agreement by which part of Marconi's company and parts of the General Electric Company came together to form the new company called Radio Corporation of America (RCA). Sarnoff was a senior manager and eventually became head of the company.

The first commercial broadcasting by radio in the United States was done by Westinghouse Electric Company in 1920. Their radio station, KDKA in Pittsburgh, carried news of the U.S. presidential election of that year.

Radio brought something new to society—a mass medium that could reach thousands of people at the same time. Delivery of a new radio to the home was a major event (see figure 4.2). Families would gather around their one radio in the living room and listen to programs together The next day at work or at school, people would talk about what they heard the night before. It was a shared experience; nothing quite like it had happened before for so many people. Radio brought people together. It also began to be an important political medium.

In 1929, the United States and much of the world sank into a deep economic depression—many businesses went bankrupt and large numbers of people lost jobs. Franklin D. Roosevelt was President of the United States from 1933 to 1945. He was one of the first major political figures to use radio as an effective way to communicate with the public. He was president during most of the great economic depression of the 1930s, when many people were frightened and discouraged by their loss of jobs, businesses, and even homes. Roosevelt began a series of radio broadcasts, which he called fireside chats, to try to raise the confidence of the citizens (see figure 4.3). A member of his staff said of him, "When his voice came over the radio, it was as though he were right [there] ... discussing [people's] personal problems with them—the cattle or crops of the farmer, the red ink of the shopkeeper, the loans of the banker, the wages of each worker."[1] Ever since, politicians have had to be good at using radio and television in order to get elected. That raised the question of whether a person's ideas and abilities were more important than his or her appearance on radio or television, an issue to this day.

Figure 4.2. *Radio and the family.* Although this is posed, it is typical of a family gathered to meet the person delivering the household's new phenomenon, a radio of the 1920s. There were some programs aimed at children, but none requiring "parental guidance." Photo courtesy of RCA.

Figure 4.3. *President Franklin D. Roosevelt talking on the radio.* In the 1930s he was the first political figure in the United States to master the use of radio to speak to his constituents, mostly by way of his weekly fireside chats.

Once a family had one radio, usually in the living room, today many homes have more than one. One, combined with an alarm clock, is in each bedroom. One is in the kitchen. Another, combined with the stereo, is in the living room or family room. There is one in the car—in fact, in each car if the family has more than one. There may be several portables for those who commute to work or school by walking, bicycling, or taking a bus or who jog for exercise. It has become a medium that we don't seem to want to be far from, even though it is no longer our primary means of entertainment or receiving news.

# Television

Imagine someone at the beginning of the 20th century trying to figure out how to send pictures by radio—and not just still pictures but moving pictures (these already existed since the 19th century). Just as the telephone represented a change from wire-based telegraphy and broadcast radio from wireless telegraphy, to create television someone would have to figure out how to get the picture into a wire so it could be sent by radio.

Early in the 20th century a Russian, Boris Rosing, had actually conceived of and built a sort of television. But it only transmitted a still image with almost no detail. He never went beyond that. Paul Nipkow, a German, developed a scanner—an early version of the television camera. An image was viewed through a small hole in a rotating disk. The disk moved, giving the viewer a sense of scanning across one line of the image, shown in figure 4.4. A person or machine peeping through the hole would see everything along one line of the image. It would be like looking at a scene through a telescope that sees only a small portion of the scene at any time but can be moved left or right to scan across the scene. When the disk reached the rightmost limit of its scan, it did not back up as a typewriter does. Instead, it let the viewer begin to peek through a new hole now just emerging at the left side of the image. The photoelectric effect (see box opposite) could convert the amount or intensity of light that came through one of these peep holes into electric current, the more light the more current. Thus, the image could be recreated at the viewing end.

Several early workers in the field realized that if television were to become a really successful medium, it would have to be all electronic. This would give greater speed and precision in scanning an image. Precision means greater resolution, or the ability to record fine distinctions among picture elements. James Baird, in Eng-

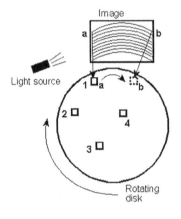

Figure 4.4. *Schematic of the Nipkow disk, the first television scanner.* An eye looking through one of the holes in this disk, then through a focusing lens, would see a small portion of the distant image. As the disk rotated, the viewer's eye would see a slightly curved strip across the image. When the peep hole got to the end of the scene on the right, viewing shifted to the next hole, just coming within sight on the left-hand side of the image. The "viewer" in this case is not a person, but a device for transmitting the amount of light seen at any spot in the image. That amount of light converted to electricity was sent to a receiver. This illustration shows just a few holes; many more were possible. It was imperfect but served for the first public broadcasts of television through the British Broadcasting Corporation.

*The photoelectric effect* converts light into electricity. If a stream of *photons* (light in particle form) strikes a surface covered with certain chemical substances, an electric current is created. This is what happens inside a television camera. Photons hit a spot on a surface within the camera and current is generated. The more light, the more current. Thus, the television system knows how much light should be seen at any one point in a scene. This knowledge is used to determine how bright a corresponding spot on the receiver should be.

land did not pursue that path. He used the Nipkow scanner to build an early TV and was able to begin broadcasting with it through the British Broadcasting Corporation (BBC) in 1929. In the meantime, in the United States Charles Jenkins, Philo Farnsworth, and Vladimir Zworykin were busily working on all-electronic televisions. They all recognized that a cathode ray tube (CRT—see box below) could serve to present the picture to the viewer. Figure 4.5 shows the concept of electronic scanning used to acquire the image for transmission. Essentially the same concept is used in a scanner for copying text or pictures into a computer, or for a photocopier or fax machine.

> *The cathode ray tube* was invented in Germany in 1897 by Karl Braun. It used an effect somewhat opposite to the photoelectric one. It used an incoming electric current to generate a stream of electrons which it could direct to any point on the inside surface of a glass tube. This surface was coated with *electroluminescent* material. Such a substance glows when struck by electrons. The more electrons at any one spot, the brighter the spot. Unless you have one of the newest TVs, with a relatively flat screen, you have a CRT in your set.

Jenkins made the first broadcast in the United States on an experimental basis. Farnsworth, with little formal education, developed some excellent equipment but was chronically short of money. Zworykin, once a student of Rosing in Russia, had moved to the United States and eventually joined RCA with Sarnoff's backing. It's interesting that Farnsworth originally told his investors it would take $25,000 to produce a working electronic television. Zworykin first told Sarnoff it would take $100,000. It actually took much more, but "the revenue would be so astronomical as to dwarf any initial outlay."[2] In 1939 the National Broadcasting Company, a subsidiary of RCA, aired the first television transmission approved by the government (see note on government regulation opposite). The first program reported on the opening of the 1939 World's Fair in New York City, with President Roosevelt trying out the new medium (see early television in figure 4.6).

Figure 4.5. *Electronic scanning of an image.* In an electronic television camera, light from the image comes into the camera and strikes a surface covered with a photosensitive substance, which generates electric current. The image is scanned line by line. A measure of the intensity of light is transmitted at any spot. In an older TV, the intensity on a line changes continuously, so you do not see pixels but you can see the lines (left image). A color camera must filter the incoming light to produce three images and transmits three sets of light intensities. Shown here are black and white images using many fewer lines than in broadcasting. The right image shows the more modern individual pixels. The farther away you stand from the image as you view it, the less you notice the individual lines or pixels. Left image courtesy of RGBQuest.com. Right image photo by the author.

*Government regulation of transmission* is needed for three reasons. First, the frequency spectrum is deemed to be in the public domain, a resource to be used in the public interest. Second, transmission is done at certain frequencies and if more than one transmitter operates at the same frequency, the signals interfere with each other, and no one would get either signal clearly. So, governments rule on who may use what frequencies. A third reason is to be sure that broadcasters do not suddenly switch their method of transmission in a way that would make the consumers' receivers useless. That was a major issue when color television was first licensed in the United States.

Figure 4.6. *An early electronic tele-vision receiver*. This Zenith model was produced in the 1940s, after World War II when TV production and consumption boomed. Photo by Richard Friedman, courtesy of the American Museum of Radio and Electricity.

By 1939 television was beginning to look not only possible but practical. Practicality meant a clear image, mechanical reliability, and a price a large number of people could afford. Unfortunately, World War II broke out in Europe that year and the United States became involved in 1941. One result was that many businesses, including RCA, turned all their energies to producing equipment needed to fight the war. In 1939 the United States was still suffering from the depression and there was not a lot of money for the average family to buy television sets. At the end of the war in 1945 companies were free to resume making products for the public rather than the Army. More people had jobs and money. Television sales soared, helped in no small way by an imaginative entrepreneur named Earl "Mad Man" Muntz, part of whose broadcast ads is shown in figure 4.7. His company produced television receivers that were simpler in design and cost much less than those of the major electronics producers. His advertising was funny and was found everywhere. For a few years, his was perhaps the biggest name in TV sales, but eventually the mainstream manufacturers caught up and Muntz went out of business. There was more and more programming available for entertainment, news, sports, and education. Pretty soon television pushed radio out of contention as the number one home entertainment medium.

Television originally broadcast only in black and white. By the late 1940s just as the industry was really getting healthy, research-ers were getting closer to making color television work (see box on p. 74) To go back a bit, John Baird had produced a form of color

Figure 4.7. *A Mad Man Muntz advertisement on television.* His ads were whacky, but he produced and sold a great many television receivers in the 1940s, when the major producers were unable to keep up with demand. Picture from the archives of the Southwest Museum of Engineering, Communication and Computation.

television as early as 1928, but it was not good enough for broadcasting. Before color really got started there was another war, this time in Korea, from 1950 to 1953. After that war color television broadcasting was finally ready and approved by the U.S. Government. Sale of receivers and broadcasting to the public began and, of course, they have been with us ever since.

Because some geographic areas could not get clear television signals due to interference from mountains or tall buildings, in 1948 there began a system of wire-based transmission in these areas. Over-the-air signals were picked up by an antenna on a tall building or mountain. They were then retransmitted over a cable that ran to every home or office in the area that chose to subscribe to the service. This arrangement was initially called *community antenna television* (CATV). Today, the signals usually go via a communications satellite to the local CATV, or now just called cable service. In many locations, almost everyone subscribes. This gives not only clearer pictures but more channels. Digital encoding of signals gives us even more channels. One hundred or more is not uncommon in major metropolitan areas.

Over the years since color came along there have been many other improvements: viewing screens are bigger, pictures are sharper, and we now get coverage of events all over the world as they happen, not days later. Thus, we saw the celebration of the fiftieth anniversary of Britain's Queen Elizabeth's coronation in 2003 in color. We see the World Cup of soccer every four years as

*Color television*. With black and white television, the scanner in the camera senses the amount of light it sees at any point of the image and sends this information to the receiver. It does not care if the color is green or blue. It cares only about the intensity of light it sees. In the receiver, a dot of light from the original image comes out white; a dark spot gets no light so it looks black. There can be many shades of gray in between.

To make color, the camera uses filters to separate light it receives by color. It then measures the intensity of light in each of three colors and sends this information to the receiver, where the three colors are combined to give the true color. The colors television uses are red, blue, and green. You are probably used to red, blue, and yellow being the primary colors and, even if you are not an artist, you can probably remember mixing paints in the primary colors to make any color you wanted. There is a difference between mixing pigments—paint—and light waves, so TV's colors work just as well. This means that there must be three separate transmissions, one for each of the colors.

The basic element of a TV image is a *pixel*, a tiny unit of color or of gray shade. In a newspaper photo, the image consists of black or white pixels, with the amount of black in any pixel varying to allow for various shades of gray. In color TV, the pixel has three parts, one for each of the colors transmitted. Each of the three may vary in intensity, but parts of all three may light up to give the resulting color desired (see figure 4.8).

the games are played in different countries. We saw the war in Iraq in 2003, not only from our own country but also from inside Iraq. Hundreds of millions of people see these major events, the World Cup being the champion in drawing viewers because of the popularity of soccer football around the world.

Is television a good thing? It certainly entertains. And it brings us news while it is happening. It can be effective in teaching. Is it a bad thing? It shows a great deal of violence, not only showing it, but perhaps making it seem that violence is the normal thing to do, especially to very young viewers. Because most of what we see is

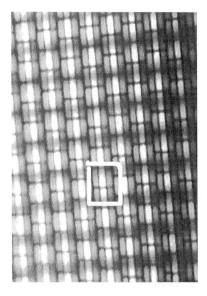

Figure 4.8. *Transmitting color.* A pixel on a modern receiver's screen consists of an array of three-part elements, one for each of the three colors transmitted. A tri-colored pixel is shown in the white oval. In each, although shown here only as shades of gray, the left-hand stripe is red, the center green, the right blue. The intensity of each stripe can vary, appearing from a distance as a single color. You can see this effect by bringing your eye close to a TV receiver and using a magnifying glass. Different models may have different arrays for the three-colored pixels, some as rectangles, some as triangular sets of three one-color elements. Photo by the author.

presented in a series of short scenes with a lot of action, children may get used to the idea that situations like those shown in stories are always simple. News tends to be a series of short announcements without much detail. We get to hear our politicians speak only for a few minutes or even just a thirty-second sound bite, which means they must greatly simplify the message they want us to hear. In 1961 Newton Minow, then head of the Federal Communications Commission (FCC) described broadcast TV as a "vast wasteland."[3]

Taken together, perhaps we forget or never learn that some things are complicated and take a lot of analysis to understand. Would we be better off going back to radio only, or to newspapers books, and magazines only? We don't really know. It's a very complicated question. We have become television people and would not easily give it up.

Has television finished growing and improving? No. We see new things every year and hear about still more. TV was once combined with the telephone, allowing it to be used to make and receive calls. That did not turn out to be popular. By installing a "set top box" or getting a brand-new set, we can receive images digitally, giving us sharper pictures and allowing us to interrupt a program, say to answer the telephone, meanwhile recording the program. On coming back we can resume viewing from the recording, which is now several minutes behind the actual transmission. We get more and more channels every year. We get bigger screens with better quality images. Will improvements ever end? Improvements to machinery of all kinds never seem to end. Are the improvements worthwhile? That's not quite so clear.

## Transistors and Integrated Circuits

Miniaturization of electronic machines came about through the invention of *transistors* and later *integrated circuits*. Radios, which now may be the size of a wristwatch, once weighed many pounds and sat only on top of a table or on their own legs. The early televisions were also weighty machines. The first electronic computers filled a room and may have needed a second room full of air conditioning equipment to cool the computer. The computers that we now carry in our brief cases or even pockets—laptops and palm-tops—run far faster and have far more memory than those room-size early machines.

An electronic circuit that runs a radio, TV, or computer needs a number of elements that can switch current to another device or amplify current. These were once electron tubes, also called vacuum tubes or electronic valves. There were typically about the size of a present-day 25- or 40-watt lightbulb, but weighed more, used more power, and generated more heat. Figure 4.9 shows the works of a tube radio of about 1950.

A great step forward was the invention of the transistor by John Bardeen, Walter Brittain, and William Shockley in 1947 at AT&T's Bell Laboratories. They shared a Nobel Prize for this work. Instead of being a vacuum tube that made use of electrons

Figure 4.9. *Tube radio.* Above is a typical radio of its time, with the case removed. It took about 30 seconds to "warm up," or be ready to run. This was an apt term since its heat could be felt even through the top of its wooden cover. As a table-top model, it was an improvement over earlier models that stood on four legs. To the right is the circuitry, seen from the bottom of the chassis. Every wire in this circuit had to be hand-inserted and connected. Photos by the author.

flowing from one point to another in a vacuum, it is a *solid state* device—one small solid object, typically about the size of a dime and perhaps 1/8 inch thick, as shown in figure 4.10. It generates very little heat and requires very little current or power. This is important in industrial and military uses where the heat could adversely affect other electronic components. The transistor began a revolution in the design of electronic machinery. Radios became something that could be carried in the pocket. Computers became about the size of an office desk and eventually book size. They are far faster than the early, vacuum tube models. Most electronic machinery became smaller, cheaper, able to be operated from relatively small batteries, and more reliable. This miniaturization required more than the transistor. In the 1950s an invention made much earlier came into widespread use—the printed circuit, one of which is illustrated in figure 4.11. It consists of a board typically made of a metal plate and a layer of plastic, epoxy, or fiberglass,

Figure 4.10. *Some transistors.* A Bell Laboratories invention, the transistor was far smaller in size than the components it replaced, used less power, created less heat, and lasted longer in service. Miniaturization began here. Its inventors won a Nobel Prize. Photo courtesy of Internet & eCommerce Online Lexikon.

to which various electronic components are attached. Wiring is done by a form of printing the wires using metal instead of ink and producing the pattern that wires might have made in older technology. The components then may be soldered to the printed wires. Such a board will be cheaper to make, much smaller and lighter than the tube-based circuits, and less subject to breakage in heavy use than the older technology.

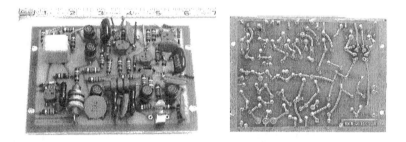

Figure 4.11. *A printed circuit board.* On the left is the top of the board, showing the various transistors and other components. On the right is the bottom of the board, showing the deposited "wires." This represented a big improvement over the hand-wired circuits, enabling many electronic devices to be made smaller, cheaper, and more reliable. Photos by the author.

Engineers are rarely satisfied for long. They began working on reducing the size not only of transistors, but of whole electronic circuits. In 1958 Jack Kilby and Robert Noyce co-invented the idea of an integrated circuit. A circuit board, such as that in figure 4.11, using transistors might typically have measured about 7.5 x 22.5 cm (3 x 8 inches). Kilby's and Noyce's innovation was to replace the entire circuit board with a single solid device, typically about 3.75 x 5 cm (1.5 x 2 inches) and .6 cm (1/4 inch) thick (figure 4.12). This is called an *integrated circuit*. Again, the size, power re-quirements, heat generated, and weight were all vastly reduced and reliability vastly increased. They enabled processors to be used not just as stand-alone computers, but also as parts of automobile engines, kitchen ovens, thermostats, and all sorts of medical devices.

Today, research scientists are working on components that are molecular in size. That would mean powerful computers could be embedded in a telephone, a microscope, or even a human brain. Imagine a world in which a telephone could not just record our messages, but understand them as well, and the human brain could store and retrieve information and do mathematics like the largest of present-day computers.

Figure 4.12. *An integrated circuit.* The reader cannot see the circuit inside the black rectangle, less than two inches wide. Co-invented at Texas Instruments and Fairchild Electronics by Kilby and Noyce, it was another giant step forward in miniaturization. Like the transistor, it reduced the power required, emitted less heat, and lasted longer in ser-vice. Its inventors won a Nobel Prize. The one shown is made by AMD and it is the central pro-cessor of a personal computer. Photo provided by courtesy of Rob Williams, www.MySuperPC.com.

# Computers and the Internet

Computers are not transmission media, but they have greatly enhanced our ability to communicate. They began to "talk" (that is, exchange information over long distances) to each other in the early 1950s, but it was relatively rare then. Transmission was through the telephone system and was rather slow, possibly as slow as 100 bits per second, compared with present day transmission speeds of 100,000 or so. Even so, the need to communicate was growing. The military (war again, this time the Cold War) needed the ability to detect incoming missiles and to control defensive forces. Research scientists, especially in computer science, wanted the ability to use programs that were written on computers in other laboratories. Businesses, schools, and hospitals were becoming decentralized, with bran ch offices in distant places. In those days a program on one computer would not necessarily run on a different computer, so research work often had to be duplicated to enable workers to make use of each other's programs. Distant communication between computers that was reliable and inexpensive enabled a person in Maryland to use a computer in California without reprogramming.

Much of the American research in computer science was sponsored by the U.S. Department of Defense (DoD). In addition to its need to control forces, the DoD had an incentive for pursuing a means by which one computer could talk to another. They wanted a user at one computer to be able to "log on" to a computer at another location and use programs in the remote machine. The initial work was sponsored by the DoD Advanced Research Projects Agency (ARPA). Some of the key developers were J.C.R. Licklider, Robert Taylor, Leonard Kleinrock, and Lawrence Roberts. What was initially developed in 1969 was called ARPANet, linking together several computers at research facilities across the United States. One by-product of this work was a way of transferring files between computers, which evolved into e-mail.

ARAPNet was highly successful and encouraged private companies to build their own networks. These allowed any computer on the network to talk with any other one on the net, mostly using telephone lines. Like a letter going through the postal system, an electronic message included the address of the destination. A small computer called an *interface message processor* (IMP) in each city could receive messages from any member computer, look at the address of the destination, and relay the message to another network computer closer to the final destination. A message might go through half a dozen or more IMPs. The original message was broken into small segments called *packets*, and each was sent through the network individually, possibly following different paths. The IMP nearest the destination put all the packets in correct order and delivered them to the destination computer. (A later packet could have gone by a shorter route than an earlier one and gotten to the destination earlier, as in figure 4.13.) Similar transmission could have been handled by one computer, in effect making a telephone call to the other which meant tying up the long distance line during all the time it might take to type an e-mail message.

It takes a tiny fraction of a second to transmit a message of 60 characters while for some users it could take a full minute to mentally compose and type the line. The network could send message traffic from a second computer while the user of the first was typing, using the time between keystrokes to send parts of the second computer's message, then the third, and so on. This cut the cost of communication to one-tenth or less of what it might otherwise have been. By now the cost reduction is considerably more.

Some computers were on more than one network, but it would have been nice if any computer could reach any other one on any network. To do that required standardization of transmission systems specifying, for example, just how the address of a message should be written. An international set of standards came into being in 1983. This is what the Internet was originally—a standard for interconnecting networks, not a network per se. Today the term is used to describe the worldwide interconnected network. There is no Internet corporation and there is no head of the Internet. It re-

## Network of computers

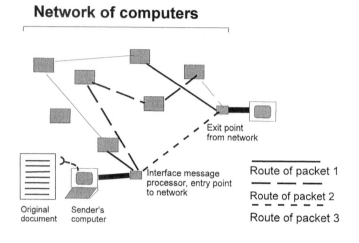

Figure 4.13. *The concept of packet switching.* A message is broken into small pieces—typically about 100 characters each—and transmitted separately to the destination. They may go by different routes, but are assembled in correct order near the destination. Note that packet 3 goes by a shorter route than packet 1, hence could arrive first. This method enables multiple users to share a communications line efficiently, saving both time and money. No time is wasted by slow typists or the sender stopping momentarily to think what to say because the time can be used to send someone else's packets.

mains a cooperative agreement among local networks worldwide. As the Internet materialized, the organizations that provided access to it, once individual networks, became known as Internet Service Providers (ISP). A user signs up with one ISP, which provides access to any other computer on the net.

# Communication Satellites

If you live in New York and see a televised football game in California while it is happening, your signals are coming to you by way of a communication satellite. The first public mention of such an invention was in a science fiction story written in 1911. Later, the British engineer Arthur C. Clarke published a scientific paper in 1945 proposing just such a thing, and then John R. Pierce, a Bell Laboratories scientist, not having seen the Clarke paper, wrote a science fiction story in 1952 involving a communication satellite. Not long after, Pierce became involved in actually building one.

What is this thing? In its very simplest form it is a satellite, an object orbiting around the earth made of a material that can reflect radio waves. The earliest human-made one was launched by the U.S. Air Force in 1958. The U.S. Navy used the moon to reflect signals from Washington, D.C., to Hawaii in 1959. Then, in 1960 came *Echo,* simply a balloon with a reflective surface put in orbit by a combination of Bell Laboratories, the Jet Propulsion Laboratory, and NASA. It enabled high-frequency radio waves aimed at it to be reflected back to earth.

Of course, a satellite has to be in just the right position to receive a signal and bounce it back to the location of the receiver. One of Clarke's ideas was that three satellites in what is called *geosynchronous orbit* (see box below and figure 4.14) would cover the entire globe. Another idea is that we don't want to merely

---

*Geosynchronous orbit (GEO).* A satellite in GEO moves around the earth at the same rate that the earth turns on its axis. Thus, relative to us, it always appears to be stationary. Think in terms of two race cars going around a curve side by side. The inner one is like a point on the earth's surface, the outer one like a GEO satellite. The outer one would have to go a bit faster than the other but, as the driver of either car looks out the side window, the other car seems always at the same relative position.

reflect the signal, we want the satellite to receive it and retransmit it back to earth. What's the difference? If you send the radio signal from an ordinary antenna, it goes out in all directions and only a small amount of the power of the signal gets to the satellite, which looks like a pinpoint from the ground. It is possible to focus the beam, getting a bigger proportion of the energy to the target, but still a lot of power is lost. Then, if whatever gets to this satellite is reflected back, the same thing happens—another loss of energy. Dr. Pierce pointed out that only one-millionth of one-millionth of one-millionth ($10^{-18}$) of the original signal makes it back to earth this way. Retransmitting at least doubles the strength of the signal that is returned to earth. Figure 4.15 shows a modern communications satellite in orbit.

In a sense, communication satellite is like a very tall tower that can receive radio signals and retransmit them. How high must the tower be? The most commonly used satellites are some 37,000 kilometers (22,300 miles) above the earth.

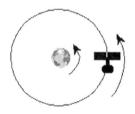

Figure 4.14. *A communication satellite in geosynchronous orbit.* The moon orbits the earth, but not *geosynchronously.* It is seen in different positions each time we look at it. A satellite that is geosynchronous is always seen at the same place above earth. Like a synchronous swimmer, it moves together with its companion astronomical body, the earth.

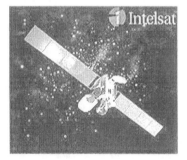

Figure 4.15. *A modern communication satellite.* Seeming to float far above the earth's surface, this satellite, launched in 2003, can handle television, messages between people, or telemetry, which is measurement data being sent from far away for processing. Photo courtesy of Intelsat Global Service Corp.

The Global Positioning System (GPS) enables a person on earth or flying above it to determine the location of its radio receiver within a few meters. The receiver may be in the hands of a hiker, explorer, lost motorist, or navigator of an airplane, small boat, or large ship. Developed by the U.S. government in 1973, this system makes use of a form of communication satellites—24 of them. It was made available for general use in 1983. The GPS receiver gets its signals from three different satellites and can tell in what direction they each are from the receiver. Using a fourth satellite, altitude can be determined—obviously of more use to aviators and mountain climbers than boat owners. Where three lines from receiver to satellite intersect is the receiver's location to within as few as three feet. Note that the lines of direction normally do not quite meet at a single point. This process is called triangulation because the lines typically do not meet at a point but create a small triangle on a map, somewhere inside of which the receiver is located as in figure 4.16.

# Wireless Telephone

When the telephone was first invented, it could be used for only one thing—voice communication between two people whose telephones were directly connected by wire. Very soon after, the exchange was invented, allowing anyone connected to the exchange to talk with anyone else who was connected to the same exchange—one wire for each subscriber, not one wire to everyone a subscriber might want to talk with. As early as 1893 the city of Budapest, Hungary, experimented with use of the telephone to broadcast news and music to all its subscribers on its network, but the idea never caught on. In the 20th century as the telegraph industry was fading out of existence, it began to use telephone lines instead of its own to send messages. The telephone became used more for voice messages and to carry telegraph and sometimes radio and television signals. In highly developed countries

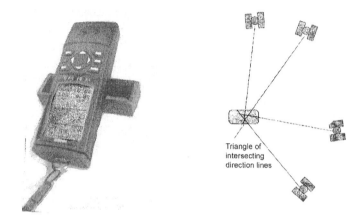

Triangle of
intersecting
direction lines

Figure 4.16. *The Global Positioning System.* At left is a typical
hand-held receiver-computer about the size of a TV remote unit.
At right is a diagram showing the GPS set receiving signals from
four different satellites whose direction from the receiver can be
measured. From this information the geographic location and
altitude of the receiver can be computed. Photo of receiver
courtesy of Elizabeth Frick.

huge networks of telephone lines evolved. For the less developed
countries, the investment required was not economically possible.

What we now call the cellular or cell phone began life in 1947
as a mobile radio connected with the telephone system. Frequencies were limited as was range and areas in which it could be used
at all. In 1979 the first modern-type cellular system was initiated
(i.e., not the older mobile radio-telephone) in Tokyo. The U.S.
government approved its use in the United States in 1982. Then
things began to change rapidly. There was the simple ability to do
away with the wire or the expensive, limited-availability mobile
radios. A telephone could now easily go with its user as he or she
traveled around a city. It did require staying within an area that
could serve cell phones and to this day that may exclude some
remote areas. Then new features began to be added and the areas

served were expanded. Today, the phones are usually called wireless or mobile telephones. Today we have many capabilities in addition to basic telephone service. Depending on the model, you might find that the phone has the following capabilities:

• It can connect with the Internet, allowing sending and receiving of e-mail. That means it also can receive radio broadcasts that use the Internet and can allow a traveler to download files from his or her own computer, which may be far away.

• It can send and receive text messages via telephone using the phone's keypad. This is different from e-mail and does not require a connection to an Internet service provider.

• It can download software: ring tones that give the user a choice from a large number of tunes, instead of the old fashioned ringing sound. It also provides linkages to computer games so games can be played through the telephone.

• It can receive pictures as well as text e-mail and, with a built-in camera, can take and send pictures as well.

• It can play recorded music and can be connected to a stereo set, allowing it to play through the stereo's multiple speakers.

• It can serve as a GPS to determine location and as a hand-held computer, doing calculations and keeping track of appointments.

• And, of course, it can use normal telephone services, such as having the phone company save incoming messages when the phone cannot be answered.

What is the difference between a modern mobile telephone with all the bells and whistles and a laptop or hand-held computer? Not much, and less every time a new model of either device comes out. The phones don't have a full-size keyboard, but it is not much of a challenge for the manufacturers to allow for an optional, detachable one.

As electronics get smaller and faster, and as more people get used to having all these services available in pocket or purse, we can expect more facilities to be added. If this tiny, multipurpose device can be a computer it can not only get a position from GPS but give us instructions as we drive on where and when to turn. It might control household devices such as a thermostat and turn off the oven that was left on when the family started on a trip.

---

Just as the telephone freed us from having to encode messages and needing a skilled operator to do so, electronics freed us from the need for wires to transmit messages over long distances and they were able to speed up the process. This is not so important when sending a voice message, but it is highly important when exchanging large files of data.

We had radio that spanned oceans and mountains, then television that sent pictures as well as sound. Then came miniaturization, not only to make our electronic machines smaller but to reduce the power needed to run them and the heat they generated and to be able to do more things for us.

Communication satellites are what enabled television signals to cross oceans and do so at a reasonable cost. These plus miniature computers gave us the Global Positioning System, slowly becoming something everyone wants in cars and boats.

Even though radio and television did not need wires to reach our homes, some areas had trouble with signals coming over the air. They might bounce off mountains or tall buildings. To counter this, cables were introduced, bringing us back to wires running into (almost) all homes and offices, but also bringing us clearer signals.

It seems that as we got comfortable with cable television we began use of wireless telephones. The latest versions of these are really computers with radios attached. They can carry voice messages, e-mail messages, and pictures. They can do calculations. They change at a rate that is hard to keep up with. What's next?

The industrial research laboratories are working on what comes next, but creative as they may be, they cannot predict what their customers are going to like. Eight-track audio tape cassettes did not make any lasting impression on our culture and 45-rpm records did not stay around for long either. There was a great conflict when video recorders and players first came out (in Japan, although invented in the United States), there was a great debate between proponents of two recording formats: Betamax and VHS (video recording system). VHS won and lasted until it has come close to being replaced by DVD, but now it turns out that Betamax was just as good. In the early 1990s SONY came out with a product that was a hand-held, hence portable, book reader, the books being recorded on disks. It was a nice machine, the size of their Walkman®, but the viewing screen was about the size of a large commemorative postage stamp. It never came to market in North America. The point is that inventors do not decide what consumers will like; consumers do, even if influenced by advertising.

# Notes

1. Rosenman, *Working with Roosevelt.*
2. Fishers and Fisher, *Tube*, p. 207.
3. Minow, "Wasteland Speech Holds True after All These Years."

# Further Reading

## General

Meadow. *Making Connections.*
Solymar. *Getting the Message.*

## Electromagnetic Waves and Spectrum

"Electromagnetic Radiation" in *Encyclopaedia Britiannica*.
"Electromagnetic Spectrum" (Web site).
Green. *Electromagnetic Radiation*.
Pierce. *Almost All about Waves*.

## Radio

Aitken. *Syntony and Spark*.
Bilby. *The General*.
Coe. *Wireless Radio*.
Kern et al. "Radio Days."
Lewis. *Empire of the Air*.
Weightman. *Signor Marconi*.

## Television

Abramson. *A History of Television*
————. *Zworykin. Pioneer of Television*.
Carpenter et al. "TV Times."
Cringley. "Digital TV" (Web site).
Garbarg. *The Economics, Technology, and Content of Digital TV*.
Fisher and Fisher. *Tube*.
Goodwin and Whannel. *Understanding Television*.
Jankowski and Fuchs. *Television Today and Tomorrow*.
"Mad Man Muntz" (Web site).
Schwartz. *The Last Lone Inventor*. (About Philo T. Farnsworth.)
"TV Screens" (Web site—good elementary description of TV picture displays.)

## Transistors and Integrated Circuits

"The Integrated Circuit" (Web site).
Reid. *The Chip*.
Riordan and Hoddeson. *Crystal Fire*.
"The Transistor" (Web site).
"Transistorized!" (Web site).

## Internet

"A Brief History of the Internet" (Web site).
Dern. *The Internet Guide for New Users.*
Wiggins. *The Internet for Everyone.*

## Communication Satellites and Global Positioning Systems

Clarke. *How the World Was Won*, pp. 197–259.
Dana. "Global Positioning System Overview" (Web site).
Hudson. *Communication Satellites.*
"Our History" (Web site. History of a major supplier of satellite
    services).
Pierce. *Beginnings of Satellite Communications.*
Roddy. *Satellite Communications.*

## Fiber Optics

Hecht. *City of Light.*

## Wireless Telephone

"Celebrating the 20th Anniversary" (Web site of Motorola, Inc.).
Lee. *Mobile Cellular Telecommunication Systems* (Technical).
Steinbock. *Wireless Horizon.*

# 5

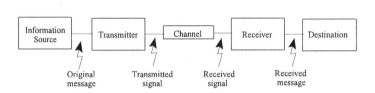

# What Is Information?
# What Is Communication?

Information . . . communication . . . the information age . . . the Internet . . . the World Wide Web . . . the media. These are now common terms we hear every day. What do they actually mean, and is it important that we know what they mean? Can't we just use them without bothering about definitions? After all, most people seem to have a pretty good understanding of what they are. Yes, most of us manage to use computers, cell phones, televisions, and radios effectively, especially when it comes to creating messages intended to have some effect on the people who receive them (or on our pets or computers). But, we often fail miserably to express ourselves in writing, to make a convincing speech, or to design a clear and effective Web site.

# Why It Matters

We have seen how the technology of communication developed; now we are going to begin to explore the basic concepts of information and communication. We will not only look at what the words mean, but how communication is done and what are some of the pitfalls in communicating effectively. We'll talk about information and data, information overload, misinformation and propaganda, messages, transmission, and media, as well as how the choice of a transmission medium affects how messages are received and understood and what happens after a message is received (what action is taken).

Information tells us what's going on in the world, and when dinner is ready. It is used to sell us things or entertain us. To be a good student, a responsible citizen, or an effective worker we need to be able to receive information and give it to others in many different ways. This is not only important for news reporters, researchers, or teachers; it is just as important for baseball players to know when a coach is signaling to steal a base or to pitch inside, for a server in a restaurant to know when a customer is signaling that she would like to give an order or get the bill, or a young person on a first date to know how to end the evening, which information may come from very subtle signals from the companion.

Let's consider a few examples. Here is a short conversation: "Who won the ball game?" "We did, three zip." Most of us would say that this is information, but we don't always realize how much a person hearing the conversation has to understand before he or she can tell what those few words meant. For example, who was playing? Which team was "we"? What does "three zip" mean? Obvious to you? It would not be to everyone. Would you answer the question the same way if you were asked by a close friend who shared your interest in sports, a visitor to your house from another country, or if you were a reporter on a national television sports news program? In each of these three cases, you would have to consider whether the person you're talking to knows who "we" are, what "three zip" means, and maybe even what game was being played. Put another way, you have to decide how best to answer the question to satisfy the particular person who asked it.

You are walking down a street and see a strange dog. It barks at you. Is there any information in that? Is the dog angry? Frightened? Is he threatening you? Or is he happy to see you and just wants to play? Can you expect that the dog would think first whether you understand his signal? You can get in trouble if you guess wrong about his meaning.

You hear on the news that a person running for mayor of your city promises to build more schools, libraries, and athletic fields if elected. Did the person really promise that, or did the person who wrote the report only *think* the candidate did, or *wish* he or she did? In either case, will the candidate really do those things if elected? What is the truth of the matter? Do you have any real information here about what is actually going to happen in the future in your city?

Finally, if you watch police stories on television or see them in the movies, you know something about what happens when people lie to the police, when well-meaning witnesses are mistaken in describing what they saw, or if the detective misinterprets some of the evidence. If you are a police officer or member of a jury, how do you decide what is true and what is not, what is information, what is a lie, and what is simply a mistake? A person's life could depend on this judgment.

Perhaps you now begin to see why it is important to analyze information, to understand how to communicate to others, and to interpret how others are trying to communicate to you. It is all too easy not to analyze the source of information or to think what is the best way to get a message across to another person. Analyzing a source means deciding how reliable that source is—a person, newspaper, or Web site, for example. What exactly do we mean by getting a message across when *we* are the source? We'll cover this in chapter 10.

Let's give some quick answers to some of these questions. In later chapters we will go into more detail.

# Information

Think about words like *news, intelligence,* and *data,* as well as *information.* Intelligence has a number of meanings, but one is something like a police officer saying, "We have intelligence that the bad guys are going to rob the bank today." In that sense, intelligence, news, and information all mean about the same thing. News implies that a message has information you did not already know. It has to be *new* and new *to you.* What if you already knew it? Say the message to the police officer on Thursday was, "Tomorrow is Friday." That's nothing new. It does not tell the officer anything not already known. It's not news or intelligence or information. Even if a newspaper or magazine gives only analysis of events, not descriptions of what happened, it may still be news. People are still discussing and debating the causes of wars and economic depressions that happened years ago. Would you buy a newspaper that only reports information you already knew, say last week's sports scores or television schedules or the results of the 1992 election?

What if you cannot understand the message? What if instead of the message about the planned bank robbery, the police received, "*xf hawf joufmmjhfodf uibu uif cbe hvzt bsf hpjoh up spc uif cbol upebz*"? It's in code. If you don't know the code, it's hardly news, intelligence, or information. It's just data. If you can break the code you can make information out of the data. (Hint: It's a substitution cipher. Each letter represents a letter in the plain-language version.) If the police can break the code, they would get two kinds of information: that the bank is to be robbed and what code is being used by the robbers. Knowledge of how to break the code means they can read future messages. This was critical during World War II when the British broke a German military code and the Americans broke a Japanese code. These two successes affected the outcome of the war. They were not just single encoded messages but code systems and the result gave the Allies the opportunity to read many messages giving much information about enemy war plans.

Data is a message we do not necessarily understand or that tells us nothing. It could be in code, in another language, or just a bunch of numbers with no explanation of how to read them and what they mean. What can a person who knows nothing about baseball or the stock market make out of a box score (figure 5.1) or the stock market tables printed in a newspaper?

**American League**

**Blue Jays 11 Tigers 0**

| Toronto | | | | | Detroit | | | | |
|---|---|---|---|---|---|---|---|---|---|
| | ab | r | h | bi | | ab | r | h | bi |
| Jhnson rf | 6 | 2 | 2 | 0 | ASnchz cf | 4 | 0 | 2 | 0 |
| Ctlnotto lf | 4 | 1 | 1 | 1 | Vina 2b | 3 | 0 | 0 | 0 |
| Hrmns lf | 1 | 0 | 0 | 0 | Infante 2b | 1 | 0 | 0 | 0 |
| VWells cf | 5 | 2 | 2 | 1 | White dh | 4 | 0 | 0 | 0 |
| CDlgdo 1b | 2 | 1 | 0 | 0 | CPena 1b | 2 | 0 | 0 | 0 |
| Berg 1b | 0 | 0 | 0 | 0 | Shelton 1b | 2 | 0 | 0 | 0 |
| JPhlps dh | 5 | 1 | 2 | 2 | CGlllen ss | 4 | 0 | 1 | 0 |
| Hinske 3b | 2 | 2 | 0 | 1 | Hggnsn rf | 1 | 0 | 1 | 0 |
| Cash c | 4 | 1 | 2 | 3 | Norton lf | 2 | 0 | 1 | 0 |
| OHudsn 2b | 4 | 1 | 1 | 1 | Monroe lf | 4 | 0 | 1 | 0 |
| Wdwrd ss | 3 | 0 | 2 | 2 | Munson 3b | 3 | 0 | 1 | 0 |
| | | | | | Inge c | 3 | 0 | 1 | 0 |
| **Totals** | 36 | 11 | 12 | 11 | **Totals** | 33 | 0 | 8 | 0 |

| Toronto | 003 | 000 | 503 | —11 |
|---|---|---|---|---|
| Detroit | 000 | 000 | 000 | —0 |

E—OHudson (2), Munson (3). DP—Toronto 3, Detroit 1. LOB—Toronto 10, Detroit 7. 2B—Catalanotto (3), VWells (5), OHudson (2), Woodward 2 (2). HR—Cash (1). CS—Woodward (1). SF—Hinske, Woodward.

| | IP | H | R | ER | BB | SO |
|---|---|---|---|---|---|---|
| **Toronto** | | | | | | |
| Halladay W,1-2 | 9 | 8 | 0 | 0 | 1 | 5 |
| **Detroit** | | | | | | |
| JJohnson L,1-2 | 4 | 5 | 3 | 3 | 1 | 1 |
| Knotts | 2 1-3 | 4 | 5 | 5 | 5 | 0 |
| Yan | 1 2-3 | 0 | 0 | 0 | 2 | 2 |
| Colyer | 0 | 3 | 3 | 3 | 1 | 0 |
| Levine | 1 | 0 | 0 | 0 | 0 | 1 |

Colyer pitched to 4 batters in the 9th. HBP—by JJohnson (Cash). T—2:37. A—17,572.

Figure 5.1. *A baseball box score.* To a person who does not know much about baseball, this message is nearly totally incomprehensible. To a person in the know, it tells a great deal about what happened in a ballgame—who did the good things, who did poorly, and, of course, who won.

Yet another view of what information is comes from the mathematical theory of communication. Claude Shannon, a noted theorist, devised a measure of information. Its use was in computing how much channel capacity was required in a particular system. Channel capacity could be bandwidth or number of bits or bytes per second that a transmitting channel would have to handle. One way to look at his work is in terms of a telegraph system that will be sending messages consisting only of codes for the letters of the English alphabet. He would find the probability of occurrence of each letter in normal usage. The letter *e* is most common in English, followed by *t, a, o, i, n*. . . . This is arrived at by repeatedly counting the frequency of occurrence of letters in various English language texts. The probability of occurrence of a letter is the number of times it occurs in a text divided by the total number of letters in that text. Call that $p$. Then, multiply $p$ by the logarithm of $p$. If you've never studied logarithms, or did but forgot, just think of it as a function—some operation performed on a number. Then, you do this for every letter in the alphabet and add up the results. That number is the number of bits of information in the system, which is the transmission channel, the alphabet in use, and the means of encoding the alphabet.[1] For the formal definition of information capacity of a channel see the box at right.

$$H = -\sum_{i=1,n} p_i \log_2 p_i$$

Here, $i$ denotes a particular letter and $n$ is the number of possible letters. The minus sign is a mathematical tactic to make the result come out positive.

Engineers would have to know how much information the telegraph company wanted to send, say in a day. Then they would devise a coding system (Morse code), and a transmission channel capable of sending the desired number of encoded letters in a day.

It's tempting to think of Shannon's measure as telling the amount of information in a message, where information is news, knowledge, or truth. He never meant that. His is an engineering measure used for engineering problems such as determining how much bandwidth is needed for use with a given type of transmission. Color image transmission uses fewer symbols per image than does black and white; sending a text message that may include Greek letters uses more different symbols than English-only.

Here are some definitions, some already discussed, that appear in the *Hyperdictionary*,[2] an online reference work:

1.  (communication theory) a numerical measure of the uncertainty of an outcome; "the signal contained thousands of bits of information."

2.  knowledge acquired through study or experience or instruction.
3.  a message received and understood that reduces the recipient's uncertainty.
4.  formal accusation of a crime.
5.  a collection of facts from which conclusions may be drawn; "statistical data."

The fourth definition was used in English law in the 19th century and is still in use, in this sense, in the United States as well.

## Messages and Signals

What exactly is a message? Another word with many meanings. Technically, in the communications world the message is the statement you *want* to send to someone else. It is information or data that has been recorded or expressed in some way. It may have been transformed from the original thoughts into written form and may have to be transformed again in order to send it over a telegraph, radio, or fax. It may have started as a written message. To become a telegram it must be converted to Morse code and then into electrical pulses sent over the wires. To become a voice radio message, it must be converted to sound, then to radio waves, and then back to sound.

Generally, the converted form of a message that is transmitted is called a *signal*. At the receiving end the signal is converted again to a message. If you have ever called a fax machine by accident on your telephone, or had one call you, the strange beeps you hear are signals. You may receive them, but you're not getting a real message unless that signal can be converted to something you can understand. Sometimes the way we understand a message is not what the sender intended. There need not have been any technical problems, but a difference between originator and destination on the meaning of the message. This is a major cause of communication problems. When a fax machine calls your voice telephone by error, it is trying to say, "I'm a fax with these characteristics. Who are you?" It wants a coded signal in return which you cannot sup-

Figure 5.2. *Man making a threat of violence.* When you see someone looking and gesturing like this, there is a clear message—at least for the moment, this is not a good person and if you are the one he is looking at, you are in danger.

ply by voice. The common parental edict, "Be home on time." is highly likely to be misunderstood, or claimed to have been.

The easiest forms that humans and most animals use to send messages are sounds and gestures. If a person stands in front of you with a club raised over his head and a nasty look on his face, as in figure 5.2, there can't be much doubt what that means. If a person holds out an open box of chocolates toward you (figure 5.3), nods, and smiles, there isn't much doubt about that either. Obviously, a printed article in a newspaper is a recorded message, as is the voice message on your telephone answering system, a song or symphony, and a painting or monument. In all these cases, the author, hold-up man, composer, or artist has some thoughts and expresses them in

Figure 5.3. *Woman making a friendly gesture.* Although fables are loaded with instances of such a gesture leading to big trouble (*Hansel and Gretel, Snow White*), in general we tend to regard this as a gesture of friendship.

spoken or written word, in gestures, in music, in a picture, or in a beautiful building. If they are not expressed somehow, there is no message and no communication. If you are not able to express yourself clearly in English—or some other language—you could not get your ideas across to other people.

So, a message is a thought recorded or expressed. The thought may be about a feeling you have. It does not have to be about something specific like how to solve a problem or what color to paint a room. The message is not the *same* as the thought. You always have to convert what you are thinking into what you are going to say or write or draw. To do that you have to know the best way to express yourself to the person or persons whom you want to receive your message, and you have to think about the best way to deliver the message to that person or those people. That brings up two important concepts: the *media of expression* and the *media for getting the message from you to them.*

# Media

*Medium* is a Latin word meaning middle. The plural is *media*. We talk about print media—newspapers and magazines—or broadcast media—radio and television. An artist may say her medium is oil paint on canvas. The medium can also be the human voice or the human voice sent through a telephone. In this sense a medium is in the middle between the person who sends the message and the one who receives it. One of the greatest writers about communication, Marshall McLuhan, is probably best known for his expression that *the medium is the message.*[3] This is a bit of an exaggeration, but he meant to stress how important the medium is in getting a message across. If you want to express support for your favorite football team during a game, you don't write team members a letter, you get everyone in the stadium yelling at once. If you want to explain some difficult concept in mathematics to students, it is probably better to carefully write it down on paper or a blackboard so they can study it when they have time. There are other meanings of media that will be discussed in chapter 9.

# Transmission

If the person you want to send a message to is not near you at the time, how do you send it? Sending a message is called *transmission*. It comes from other Latin words meaning *sending across*. If you have a friend in another city, the method of transmission might be e-mail, telephone, or writing a letter to be sent through the post office. Other means of transmission are or have been: having a traveler carry a letter, perhaps on horseback as with the Pony Express, sending smoke signals as the peoples of the American Plains did, sending fire signals as Paul Revere's friend did at the start of the American Revolution, sending signals by drum as did various peoples in Africa, putting a note in a bottle and dropping it into the ocean for the currents to deliver, or carving the words in stone as we find in many public buildings and monuments. This last method is important because it is an attempt to transmit to people who are not distant in space but distant in time. Archaeologists often find and understand inscriptions carved as words or pictures on buildings thousands of years ago, such as in the Egyptian pyramids.

We call the person who decides to send a message the *source* or *originator* and the one who receives the message the *recipient* or *destination*. What happens if, for any number of possible reasons, the message the recipient gets is not what the originator intended to send? We'll describe some of these reasons later. Most of the effort in communication is spent trying to make sure that the recipient does get and understand the message that the originator intended. That means taking care in composition to express thoughts well, thinking about how the recipient will react, and thinking about the transmission medium. You would not send the same message in a letter as you would on television.

## Communication

What does the word *communication* mean? We say things such as, "I was in communication with her last week," or "He communicates well." Is there a difference between communication and transmission? People who work in communications tend to feel that communication requires that a message or messages must not only be sent but also be received. In that sense, transmission *is not* the same as communication. You can send a letter that is never received. You can shout a message to a person who cannot hear you. You can ask a polite question in English of a person who speaks only Japanese and who therefore will not understand you. The Japanese person may have heard you—received the signal—but not understood you. It's like the fax machine on the telephone—another case of getting the signal but not the message.

In the technical sense, the terms *communication* and *transmission* may be synonyms. In the social sense they are not— communication tends to require understanding as well as receipt of a message. When we speak of a person who is a good communicator we mean someone who can express himself or herself well, which means not only putting ideas into words but knowing what words are going to be understood by the audience and how they will be understood. You may have left a message on someone's telephone answering machine and never heard back. That means, for whatever reason, you may not have communicated with the person, only with the machine. It is not uncommon for parents and children to misunderstand each other, even if there is an exchange of messages. As with the telephone answering system, there is no communication because the various messages were not understood by the intended recipient or were perhaps just ignored. Figure 5.4 shows a simplified diagram of the communication process first used by Claude Shannon. Note that this shows that communication involves more than composing messages. They must be transmitted *and* received as well.

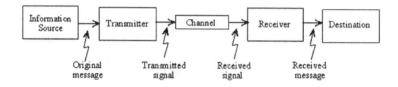

Figure 5.4. *Shannon's model of the communication process, simplified.* The basic elements are: an *originator,* who creates the message and can be human, animal, machine, or even plant; a *channel,* which transports the message; a *transmitter,* which converts the originator's message into a form that can be transported such as sound into electric current; a receiver, which takes the message from the channel and converts it again into a form that can be understood by the *destination,* which again can be a human or other kind of entity.

Chapter 4 described President Roosevelt's use of radio. He was the first in the United States to be an effective politician in the use of radio and was able to calm the fears of Americans about the economic depression. John F. Kennedy was a stellar performer on television, "vanquishing the camera-challenged Richard Nixon"[4] in 1960. President Reagan was another who knew how to use the visual media effectively. Today, John Madden broadcasts professional football games on television. He sometimes jokes about his not understanding big words, but his speech is colorful, he knows the game well, and he knows how to explain what is happening. All these men are examples of great communicators. Other modern people who know how to use the television medium well are Oprah Winfrey and Jon Stewart. By the time we got to 1994, we had a new medium that commanded attention—the World Wide Web. It was used for the first time very effectively in the 2004 presidential primary campaign by a previously not well-known candidate, Governor Howard Dean. Other politicians quickly took notice of Governor Dean's early success in raising funds and gaining supporters.

A great interviewer on radio or television has to keep both the person interviewed and the people listening in mind and constantly work to get the interviewee to explain, to use understandable language, and to be concise. In short, the interviewer is a content editor, assuring that the message is going to be understood by the destination. Further, the interviewer has to control the use of time without really seeming to be watching the clock. Jim Lehrer and Gwen Ifill on PBS and Tim Russert on NBC are TV interviewers who are well able to get the story out to the viewer.

## Noise

Noise is one of the main problems encountered in communication. In the communications world, noise does not just mean an unpleasant sound, it means any signals received that were not intentionally sent by the originator. Yes, noise can be a loud sound such as the background noise in a crowded restaurant when you are trying to talk with someone. It can be a cell phone ringing in a theater auditorium during the show. It can be static on a radio or telephone caused by electromagnetic waves from a passing airplane or large truck. It can be a television image speckled with spots or one reflected off a mountain or tall building, thus giving the receiver two slightly offset versions of an image. The latter is called a ghost image. Figure 5.5 shows a noise-free image and figures 5.6 and 5.7 show the two main forms of noise distortion. Designers of transmission systems always have to worry about what can cause noise and how to prevent or minimize it. There will be more on this in chapter 9.

---

I have tried to make clear the meanings of some of the key words in the communication field, as well as to show why it is important to know what they mean. A final point before I get into more detail: People normally want and expect messages communicated

Figure 5.5. *Television image without noise.* Noise is not just unpleasant sound—it is anything that, added to a signal, may interfere with reception or under-standing. Shown here is a the noise-free image of well-eroded rocks in a desert.

Figure 5.6. *Noise in the form of "snow."* This figure shows the previous image with some noise imposed in the form of random specs.

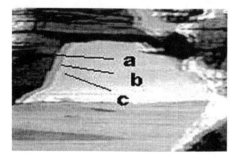

Figure 5.7. *Noise in the form of ghost images.* Here, enlarged, we see an edge in the original image at a, another version is at b and, barely visible, still another at c.

to them to be true. Are they always true? How can we tell? What do we mean by true? That last question is difficult to answer because there are so many different answers to it and it is not fair or nice to say, "Oh, no. Your meaning of truth is not right. You have to use *my* meaning." So, is everything we read in the newspapers or books, hear on the radio, or see on television or the Internet true? Do people ever intentionally send false messages? Is a message that is not true an intentional lie? These are all difficult questions. There are few good answers.

# Notes

1. Shannon and Weaver, *The Mathematical Theory of Communication*, pp. 3–4.
2. Definition of "information" in *Hyperdictionary* (Web site).
3. McLuhan and Fiore, *The Medium Is the Message*.
4. Rich, "Napster Runs for President."

# Further Reading

## Information, Communication, Messages, and Signals

Cherry. *On Human Communication*.
McLuhan. *Understanding Media*.
Meadow. *Making Connections*.
Penzias. *Ideas and Information*.
Shannon and Weaver. *The Mathematical Theory of Communication*.
Weaver. "Some Recent Contributions."

## Media

Brand. *The Media Lab*.
Briggs and Burke. *A Social History of the Media*.
McLuhan. *Understanding Media*.
Negroponte. *Being Digital*.
Vivian. *The Media of Mass Communication*.

# Transmission and Noise

Schwartz. *Information Transmission, Modulation and Noise.* (An advanced text)

Chandler. "The Transmission Model of Communications" (Web site).

Weaver. "Some Recent Contributions."

# 6

# Different Views of Information

Now we are going to look deeper into those questions about what information is, in what varieties it can be found, whether information is always true or a true message always contains information, and whether entertainment is or contains information. Basically, we'll consider the idea that to be information a message has to change the person, animal, machine, or system of any kind that receives it. Note that this does not say that anything that changes a system is information. A good, hard right hook from a boxer can change the opposing boxer and in that sense does convey information about the opponent or the recipient's judgment in agreeing to this fight. A more limited definition would be that information must change what we will call the *knowledge base* of the recipient. A broader one is that it change the knowledge base or *feelings* of the recipient.

# Information and Data

Let us start with the difference between data and information. Some scientists define information as *a signal that changes its recipient*. Some define it as that which reduces uncertainty in the recipient—certainly a form of changing the recipient. *Data do not cause this kind of change.* Such a definition fits better in physics or engineering where the recipient under consideration is a machine or some purely physical entity—no feelings or knowledge needs to be involved. The change may not be beneficial, but the fact that it happens means that the received signal has been processed somehow and combined in some way with existing knowledge or state. On the other hand, data consists of just *a stream of symbols*, unprocessed or incompletely processed, not understood, and not integrated or assimilated by the destination.

Already we have something of a problem because I use the word *information* sometimes as a general word and sometimes as a form of message that is different from data. Sorry, that's a problem that exists throughout the information science world. Everyone seems to use some of the most basic words in different ways. But when scientists take the time to make careful definitions, they tend to use the meanings that are used in this book. Informally, they also tend to keep on using the word *information* in more than one way, as I do.

Historically, the word *information* comes from the Latin word *informare*, which means to give form to, shape, mold, or fashion, according to the *Oxford English Dictionary*. That pretty much fits with our modern idea of the verb *form,* which implies creating or shaping something. One of the oldest recorded uses in English comes from Geoffrey Chaucer's *Canterbury Tales*, which he began writing in 1387 and was incomplete when he died in 1400. Spelled *informacion* or *informacioun*, the word seems to mean more or less what we generally use it to mean today—less of physically shaping something and more of giving news or instruction. Today, we have a science of information and we try to give terms exact meanings. We mentioned *news, intelligence*, and *data*, which are common, generally understood words today. Claude Shannon's mathematical definition was mentioned in chapter 5. To be really precise and to be understood when talking about information, the meaning of the word *information* you are using has to be made clear.

## Attributes of Information

While we prefer the definition of information as something that changes the state of its recipient, sometimes it simply refers to an object such as a book, a stock market tip received through e-mail, or a set of driving directions. It can also be an intangible, such as an oral message. Some information serves only to tell about other information, for example the words in fine print in boxes on many application forms that say NAME or TELEPHONE NUMBER. There is information there explaining what the content of the box is. This has come to be called *metadata*. It has virtually no value in itself but is important in understanding other information, namely the contents of the box.

Whichever definition we use, information has value and there are several meanings of this word, too. One meaning of value is *price*. When you bring an object across an international border, the customs people want to know its value, which to them means price. Another meaning is *imputed value*, which is a value someone thinks something is worth. If I learn how to transmute lead into gold, I may offer my formula for a certain price. Since it has never been sold before, there is no established price. I would just be saying what I think it should be worth, Finally, there is *sentimental value*, often mentioned in advertisements for recovery of lost items. My grandfather's watch, even though it does not run anymore, is worth a great deal to me but very little to anyone else.

What is the value of an item retrieved from a search on the World Wide Web? The point just made is that it can be quite different for different people, or it can be different for the same person at different times. If we could transmute lead into gold, it might so affect the market for gold that we cannot predict the value of the invention, and it might be that, as the market price of gold approaches that of lead, the demand for it disappears. When searching the Internet, we sometimes place a high initial value on the first item retrieved that is on the desired subject. More searching may uncover much better documents, making us change our initial valuation. It can work the other way, too. An item may initially be rated as C or so-so, but when we find nothing better we might change the grade to an A.

## Content and Context

A message has *content*. Its content is what it means, what it says to the person receiving it. The content may be the score of a game, the price of something you want to buy, a question ("How do I get to Main Street?"), or the answer to the question. If the content is not understood by the person who receives the message, then communication has not been achieved. If you get the message, "I'll meet you at eight," you may have thought it meant 8 PM, while the person who sent the message meant 8 AM. Even though you technically received the message, you don't know what time the meeting was intended, although this was the main point of the content. There was some communication, but it was not effective because the recipient might not show up at the right time.

Suppose you and a friend regularly meet on Wednesday evenings to work, study, or play squash together at the usual time, 7 PM. Then the message, "I'll meet you at eight," probably means 8 PM, meaning that the usual meeting is to be delayed by an hour. If a major change was intended, it is reasonable to assume the sender would have said more, such as, "Let's make it at eight in the morning." If you know that your friend usually has a commitment at 7 AM, you can be even more sure that an evening meeting was suggested. To you the message now has meaning. To someone else who may have seen it, the message is still unclear. Context, once generally defined as the relationship of a word or phrase to its surrounding text, now is often defined in terms of the relationship of any text to a broader situation. That might mean the state of world politics or of an unwritten understanding between business associates. In the context of the message about a meeting, it does not tell a third party who is meeting whom and does not clearly tell when. The same thing happens if you pick up the stock market listing in the newspaper. Unless you study the market, these numbers are probably quite meaningless, but if you're a stock broker, or even just have a hobby of keeping up with the market, it is all quite clear. The point is that the difference between data and information depends on who is reading the message and what that person knows both about the world and about the sender.

## Knowledge and the Knowledge Base

Another way to look at the difference between data and information is that how you interpret a message depends on what you already know when you get it. One philosopher said, "All human knowledge takes the form of interpretation."[1] If you cannot interpret it—make sense of it—it's data.

Some other views include one by Samuel Johnson, who pointed out that, "Knowledge is of two kinds. We know a subject ourselves, or we know where we can find information upon it."[2] The second sense is essentially what we now call metadata or metaknowledge. Yet another variation on information is to point out that we can know *about* something or know *how to do* something, which includes how to find information. Plato has Socrates ask the question amidst a long discourse about knowledge," . . . [is knowledge] true opinion accompanied by reason?"[3] His question, as usual, suggests an answer: When forming an opinion, based on thinking about current knowledge or receiving a new message, it is essential to process the thought, to think about it, to correlate it with existing information in one's mind.

Christopher Fox and others[4] used the expression *justified true belief* for knowledge. What we think of as knowledge is something we believe to be true, whether it is the relationship of the radius to the circumference of a circle, integrity (or lack thereof) of a politician, or the meaning of life. But true belief must be justified, and there's the rub. There really cannot be an objective standard for justification; whether we are talking about the credibility of a newspaper article or of religious teachings, we all have our own bases for justifying our belief in the truth of the matter.

Information scientists have taken to calling the total of what any one person knows that person's *knowledge base* (KB). Or it could be a machine, computer, or computer program. Your KB is different from mine. It is probably more likely that two persons have the same fingerprints than that they know exactly the same things, neither one knowing anything the other does not. Most formal definitions of a knowledge base are stated in terms of computers and artificial intelligence, but people, too, have know-ledge bases. An alternative and broader definition of knowledge base is "the content of a particular domain or field of knowledge."[5]

There is a lot of talk these days about clones. A clone is a biologicall y identical copy of a living thing, whether a plant, an animal, or even a person. While we might be able to clone a person we cannot possibly create a new person identical in all respects to another because the clone would grow up in a different environment. The parents or guardians would be different (perhaps just older), the friends would be different, the whole world would be different. The clone could not possibly know exactly what its parent knows. He or she (or it?) may know more than its parent about genetics, but its knowledge base and its parent's knowledge base cannot be identical. Hence, the context of a received message may seem different to the clone than to its parent.

Since no two people have exactly the same knowledge base, we are once again reminded how important it is to think how a message might be received and then to think how best to assure that it is understood. During World War II the U.S. Army sometimes used Navajo soldiers as voice radio operators. They could speak in plain language; no need to encode. How many Europeans or Japanese who might have intercepted the message could have understood the language? What counted was knowledge that the intended recipient would know Navajo but enemy soldiers would not.

In line with trying to define key terms, some scientists define information as a message that changes the knowledge base of the recipient of the message. Others say it's information if it changes the system that receives it in some way without being specific about a knowledge base. Take one of the simplest of our modern-day machines, a ballpoint pen, as an example. There are several kinds, but one has a button at the top. Press the button once and the point is pushed out, ready to write. Press the same button again and the point retracts so it doesn't mark your hands or pocket. The message, "The button has been pushed," changes the system but how it changes it depends on the condition, or state, of the pen—that is, what the pen "knows"at the time. We could say it's the pen's knowledge base that changes, that the pen knows very little but it does know what state it is in and acts accordingly. See figure 6.1. There are many other examples: push a button once to turn on power on many electrical machines, once again for power off. The device you are controlling "knows" what to do and does something different each time.

Figure 6.1. *A ballpoint pen—a machine with a brain?* The pen is not very smart, but it does know what to do when you send the only message possible, pressing the button. Its decision is based on its quite meager knowledge base, consisting of knowledge of what state it is in currently.  Photo by the author.

But was that push of the button a message containing a symbol or, like the earlier example of the boxer's right hook, a physical blow, not a recorded symbol? One of the techniques of the science of cybernetics is to treat a system as a "black box," an organism whose internal workings we do not necessarily know. However, if we can define all the possible states of the system and know all its possible inputs, we can describe the system in terms of how it reacts to a given input or stimulus. By *react* we mean change its state or send a message (a form of changing state). It is in that sense that the right hook is an input or a stimulus or a message.

Remember the example of the person raising a club over his head and glaring at you. You would learn something from that—the message does not need words. You know that person is dangerous to you, not just now but probably in the future, too. If you hear a piece of music that is new to you, what have you learned? It is hard to say exactly, but you might have been changed in some way—made happier, sadder, more excited. The musical message could change you to some extent.

We can say that knowledge is an accumulation of all the information you ever received and retained in some form. But knowledge is more than just a mental file cabinet full of messages. Knowledge implies you have not only received many messages in your lifetime in many different forms, but you have managed to decide which to assimilate and then done it. Assimilating information means relating it to what you already know, making the new information part of your knowledge base. Once again, a message that is not assimilated is not information. At best it is data. Assimilation, by the way, requires time, even if measured in milliseconds or microseconds. There is, therefore, a limit to how much we can assimilate in a given period of time.

## Information Overload

This difference between data and information is what is at the heart of the concept of information overload. That expression is generally taken to mean that today we are faced with too much information, more than we can cope with. But information is what we bring into ourselves, *understand*, and have it change us. If it does all this, where's the overload?

There is no known limit to the amount of information a human being can assimilate. The only way we can have an overload is if there *appears* to be more data, which is potentially information, than we can handle. We may receive the message in the technical sense but have not been able to do the work of assimilation. Or we might understand the gist of the message but reject it as unimportant because we did not comprehend all the detail. Then, the part we did not assimilate is not really information, it remains merely data.

Is this just a semantic game, playing with word definitions? No, it is not. Almost since writing—recording information—began there has been more of it than a person can read and assimilate. The ancient Greek library at Alexandria, Egypt, in the 3rd century CE, had been variously estimated to have some 20,000 to 700,000 scrolls. The true number is still unknown. Even at the rate of one book a day, it would have taken over a hundred years to read them all and, of course, during that century there would be hundreds or thousands more written.

So the essence of this overload problem is selection. What do we choose to read or not to read? The Internet search engine Google scanned more than five billion Web site pages in 2005 and grows steadily. No one could possibly read that much, so we must rely on Google, recommendations from others, or our own good sense to decide which of that vast number of items we are going to read and accept as true or useful. The situation can certainly be stressful. The person involved may feel there is more information that is needed but has not yet been found or feels guilty for not having found it. In either case, the problem is not too much information; it is that we don't know how much there is or how to find it, or even whether any of the unread messages actually contain information. That causes stress.

# Learning

Closely related to knowledge is *learning*. As a noun, it means the same as knowledge—what we know. As a verb, learning may be considered as the process of receiving and assimilating new information. We all know that we can sit in a classroom, church, or political hall, hear a speaker talk, but daydream through it all and learn nothing. Just having biologically heard the message is not enough. We can listen to a coach tell us how to hit a baseball, but as the great Ted Williams once said, to hit a round ball coming toward you at 80 to 100 miles an hour with a round bat is the hardest task in sports.[6] It requires learning to know when to swing and exactly how to move all the various muscles involved in swinging the bat. You learn to do it mostly by trial and error. Coaches can help by telling you how to stand and hold the bat, but your own body sends you messages about how and exactly when to swing, and your knowledge base stores away the information about what worked best the last few times. The knowledge of how you swung the bat and what effect it had comes from yourself. No one tells you about it by e-mail. It came from your eyes and your sense of feel. Maybe even from your ears because ball players often know they have hit a home run by the sound of the bat hitting the ball, long before the ball reaches the far distant fence.

# News and Intelligence

News is generally thought of as information that is new. If it is not new, there is no learning and no change to our knowledge base. We may have heard the message a hundred times, but it didn't sink in. If we hear it the 101st time and it *does* sink in, it became news to us. Once again, we have to realize that what is new to one person may not be to another. Newspapers and news programs on radio and television generally report information that is new to most readers. If they did not, they would soon have few readers or listeners. But on a slow news day, you may hear or see yesterday's headlines rehashed.

We also mentioned intelligence. One meaning of intelligence has to do with how smart you are or even how smart your dog is. In animals, one way to measure intelligence is to see how easily they learn new things and how many words or commands they seem able to learn. In people, the meaning of intelligence is far more complex and includes both what you know and what you can do with the knowledge you have, such as solve problems. But in our context we are more interested in the military meaning. In the army, intelligence is information usually about an enemy, so it is exactly what we have been calling information.

## Disinformation

During the World War II (1939–1945), the Allies—mostly American, British, and Canadian armies—were preparing to invade France, which was then occupied by soldiers of Nazi Germany. It was important not to let the Germans know where the invasion would take place. Elaborate schemes were worked out to try to provide false intelligence to steer the defenders away from the actual place where the troops would go ashore. The schemes worked. The defenders were not ready for the actual landing in the Normandy region of France; they assumed it would be elsewhere, near the city of Calais. There are lots of other examples in history of such *disinformation* or lies intended to fool someone, perhaps with the intent of accomplishing something good as a result. If we receive a false message but believe it and act on it, it has changed our knowledge base. Is it information even if it is not true?

Around 800 BCE most of the people of Israel were taken into captivity in Babylon. Some were left behind in Jerusalem. In the Jewish religion a new month begins with a new moon, the first day that a tiny part of the moon can be seen after shrinking to nothing following a full moon. It can be difficult to tell just by looking on which night the new moon falls. There is very little difference from one day to the next so it's easy to be off by a day. The people left behind in Jerusalem used to signal to those in Babylon when the new moon came to be sure the captives knew exactly when to celebrate. The message was transmitted by a sheaf of dried stalks and sticks set afire and waved in a particular pattern as in figure 6.2. This was done on top of a mountain and the signal could be seen on top of the next mountain where it was repeated to the next mountain, and so on from Jerusalem all the way to Babylon, some 800 kilometers (500 miles) away. Some members of the Samaritan sect tried to send false signals. They would send a similar signal on the wrong night, a very early example of disinformation. To the people on the receiving end, a signal one day early or late would still seem true. The solution to avoiding disinformation, we are told, was to send a messenger, instead of the fire signal. Actually, the messenger could not have made the trip in one day. This was a case where speed of transmission was of utmost importance.[7]

Figure 6.2. *Sending gestural signals to Babylon.* It was important for the Israelites in Jerusalem to signal to those in Babylon when the new moon occurred, which was important for ritual events. The originator waved a sheaf of burning straw in a particular pattern. This was picked up and repeated at a relay point.

One defense against a form of disinformation is what anthropologists call the *costly signaling theory*, which can explain both why some messages may be difficult to fake and how some groups of people create strong bonds among the members.[8] The example of the Israelite fire signals was one of a signal that was easy to fake. The bonds that tie together members of a religion or of a secret society like the Masons are not so easy to fake because a great deal of effort has to go into learning the particular behavior (for ex- ample, a secret handshake, avoidance of certain foods at certain times of the year, wearing clothing that may be uncomfortable, frequent attendance at rituals). These require a great deal of effort and, sometimes, of physical pain, as in some initiation ceremonies. The harder it is to learn to become a member, the more likely it is that someone who learns to send them is, to other members, truly a person who can be trusted. A more mechanical example is paying extra money to use coaxial cable instead of plain, uninsulated wire. Actually, one of the principles of coax cable—putting a metal sheath around a wire—is used to prevent electromagnetic radiation from escaping from a room where secret materials are being used. Ordinary computers unintentionally send out some electromagnetic waves, which can be intercepted and interpreted by a vigilant and well-financed spy. In a sense, all this may be viewed as a form of redundancy used to combat ordinary noise in transmissions. In the case of secret rituals, "redundancy" is in the form of extra rules to be obeyed (and seen to be obeyed), extra expense, extra time for various forms of devotion, or endurance of physical pain, all of which help to assure that only the members of the group are accepted as such and trusted by other members.

# Truth

The question about what is true gets us into philosophy and possibly religion. Many people believe their own is the one true religion. Nothing is wrong with that. They may not necessarily say others are false, but that those others are mistaken or uninformed or simply that all believers are free to see things their own way. To many of us that means we have to accept the idea that a message can be true for one person or group and not for another. That would mean that we tend to treat a message as true if it is consistent with everything else we know, everything that is part of our knowledge base, and is false if it contradicts what is in our knowledge base. We must be careful with this. Our knowledge base may be sophisticated enough to recognize a contradiction and trigger a response that does not automatically reject the new message but indicates a need to verify it and maybe even revise our previous thinking. But if we are not so sophisticated we might retain all sorts of contradictory notions.

We frequently read about new developments or theories in science. Can it be that carbon dioxide released from burning certain fuels ultimately causes some of the erratic climatological changes of recent years? For many, this is hard to believe. But the challenge of adding new beliefs to our base of accepted knowledge is not new. An ancient Greek, Democritus, who lived in the 5th century BCE believed that the world was made up of four elements: earth, air, fire, and water. He proposed that there was a smallest particle of any element called an atom. Nothing smaller than an atom was still the same substance. Today, we know that each of his original four elements is made up of several others and that there are actually 112 basic chemical elements. How many people in those days had ever seen or felt hydrogen or even suspected it existed? How many today know from direct experience that the element californium exists? Even today, how many know from personal experience that there are atoms of elements that are not divisible in the sense that dividing one does not yield smaller portions of the same element? Overwhelmingly, most of us get such knowledge from books or lectures from sources we trust. It was not always easy to get people to accept Democritus' theory as truth, but over the years we all have come to accept that atoms exist and are indivisible in the sense that half an iron atom is no longer iron. We have, however, come to reject Democritus' theory of four elements.

The Polish astronomer Copernicus proposed the theory that the earth revolves around the sun, not the other way around. This, too, was not easy even for educated people to accept. We still talk about sunrise and sunset as if the sun moved around the earth rather than the other way around. But by now almost everyone accepts that the earth is moving, not the sun, and more recently, we came to accept that the earth moves relative to the sun, which is also moving relative to other heavenly bodies. In 1859 Charles

Darwin proposed that biological species, including humans, evolved from other species. That caused quite a stir as many people did not like to be considered descended from apes. (He never said they were.) Others felt it contradicted a literal interpretation of the Bible. All these new ideas when first proposed were not consistent with most people's knowledge bases, but as ever more evidence—messages from reliable sources—came along, knowledge bases began to change and most, but not all, modern people now accept all these ideas.

The so-called urban myths are an example of a type of message whose truth we do not know upon receipt. Basically, they are stories often attributed to a friend that are interesting, sometimes funny, sometimes horrifying. But they cannot easily be verified, which does not, in itself, make them untrue. I heard such a story once, well, twice, from two different people whom I did not think knew each other, but both were allegedly friends of one of the people involved. It was funny and could easily have happened. But when I heard the same story a second time from a different person, I began to have doubts. Reports of computer viruses and actions that everyone is advised take to overcome them tend to circulate among e-mail recipients. They tell about a new virus and urge us to delete a certain file from our computer. Unfortunately, the file is one little known to most computer users but necessary to operation of the computer. The helpful letter is completely false but attributed to someone "in the know" in a company where people should know these things. The point of all this? Determining truth is not an easy matter.

Does a message have to be true to contain information? How do we decide what is true? The purpose of communication is not to demonstrate truth; it is to deliver a message that is understood as its source intended it be understood. If a student is writing an exam paper, an answer is intended not to enlighten the teacher but to show how much the student knows about the given topic. The answer to the question may be false, but nonetheless shows the truth about what the writer knew.

How do you come to have faith in a source or in a scientific test procedure? Generally, you have learned from experience that a person, publication, or broadcaster tells the truth or because someone that you trust encouraged you to believe in the source. Many of us learn from our parents which newspapers to believe or which political party to believe in. In judging popular music, we tend to learn from our peers or friends just a little older than we are, *not* from our parents. We may change our minds as we grow older and decide to receive other messages from other sources. So, even if we cannot define truth, we know that we will believe some messages—take them to be true—if they come from a source we trust. And we will distrust a message that comes from a source we believe to be unreliable or often wrong.

The point of all this is that two people can receive the same message and to one it is true information and to the other it is not. If you are the person sending a message you must find some way to make sure your message will be accepted as true.

## Propaganda and Misinformation

Another aspect of the question of truth is *propaganda*. This word used to mean the propagation or spreading of ideas, including good ideas, but now it usually means distorting the truth or modifying it in order to support a particular point of view. Sometimes even the nicest governments do it to gain support for some policy or action of theirs. Sometimes private companies or trade organizations do it to create good feelings toward themselves by the public or to oppose some government policy. Commercial advertising is essentially propaganda. People are told how great the product is, even if it is not actually great, but pictures of happy, attractive people using it make us feel good about it and want to buy it. Propaganda has to be believable to be effective. It has to sound like truth to reasonable people.

Disinformation is usually an outright lie, like letting an enemy know or think we are planning to invade at Calais instead of Normandy. What we call misinformation tends to be more subtle—half truths or something unintentionally wrong. In 2003 the United

States government was of the opinion that weapons of mass destruction were to be found in Iraq. Subsequently, this turned out not to be true. Were the government's messages to its people disinformation—something intentionally false—or misinformation—a mistake honestly made?

What it all comes down to it is that if you believe it, propaganda or misinformation is information to you. If you cannot believe it then it may become information of a different sort. When someone lies to you, whether a friend, a government, or a company, and you know what you are hearing is a lie, then you have information. Unfortunately, the information you have is that someone or some organization that you may have trusted is not really trustworthy. At any rate the message changes you and therefore is information. I will discuss the important process of evaluating information or a message in chapter 11.

Some misinformation is caused by noise, an unintended signal. Static on a radio or telephone can easily cause words to be misunderstood by the recipient. More about noise is found in chapter 9.

## Entertainment as Information

Some messages are not meant to inform you or convince you or lie to you. They are simply meant to entertain you, or to provide a sense of beauty (as music or painting), or to stir you up (as a school's "fight" song or a national anthem). Do these messages carry information? Somewhat like the boxer's right hook, such a message is not necessarily meant to provide new facts but is intended to change the recipient and it comes more in concrete than symbolic form.

If we use the definition of information that it is a message that changes the recipient, then, yes, entertainment and art can be information. If you are made to feel good from watching a comedy on television, or sad from watching a drama, or if you feel elated from seeing a picture or hearing something beautiful, then you have been changed, even if only temporarily. And so the communication of entertainment can convey information.

---

What has been brought out in this chapter is that the word *information* has several meanings as it is commonly used. One meaning is *data*, a message that is meaningless to the recipient or tells nothing new. Another meaning is that information is a message that changes the *knowledge base* of the recipient. A new information-carrying message has to be *assimilated* into that knowledge base. This means it must be related to what is already known, not merely stored away like a card in a file.

We considered *truth* and the important question of whether a message has to be true to be information. The best answer I can provide to that question is that the recipient has to believe it is true *or* that the false message says something about whoever sent it.

I described propaganda and misinformation, intentionally misleading messages. Finally, I showed that entertainment messages can change us and so should be considered to have information.

In the next chapter I go into messages; how information is represented in them and to what extent the medium of transmission—the way they are sent—affects the meaning.

# Notes

1. Walter Benjamin, cited in *Columbia Dictionary*.
2. Boswell, *Life of Samuel Johnson*.
3. Plato, Theaetetus, p. 49.
4. Fox et al, "Foundational Issues in Knowledge-based Information Systems."
5. Definition of "information" in *Hyperdictionary*.
6. "A Visit with Hall of Famer Ted Williams" (Web site).
7. *Mishnah*, p. 189.
8. Sosis, "The Adaptive Value of Religious Ritual."

# Further Reading

## Information and Data

Buckland. *Information and Information Systems*.
Definition of "knowledge" in *Hyperdictionary* (Web site).
Definition of "knowledge" in *The Free Dictionary* (Web site).
Definition of "knowledge" in *WordIQ* (Web site).
Marchionini, *Information Seeking in Electronic Environments*, pp. 1–8.
Meadow et al. *Text Information Retrieval Systems*, pp. 34–43.

## Knowledge and the Knowledge Base

Keegan. *Intelligence in War*.
Meadow et al. *Text Information Retrieval Systems*, pp. 43–46.
"The Nature of Knowledge" in *Encyclopaedia Britannica*.

## Alexandria Library

Innis. *Empire and Communications*, p. 92.
Kilgour. *The Evolution of the Book*, p. 44.

## Learning

Domjan and Grau. *The Principles of Learning and Behavior*.
"Learning" in *Encyclopaedia Britannica*.

## News and Intelligence

Budiansky. *Battle of Wits*.
"Intelligence" in *Encyclopaedia Britannica*.
Keegan. *Intelligence in War*.
Mackesy. *The Searchers* (Radio Interception).
Williams and Lipetz. *Covert and Overt*.

## Propaganda, Misinformation, and Disinformation

Breuer. *Deceptions of World War II.*
————. *Hoodwinking Hitler.*
Chomsky. *The Spectacular Achievements of Propaganda.*
"D-Day" (Web site mentioning of deception in WWII Normandy landings).
"Department of Defense News Briefing" (Web site on disinformation).
Ellul. *Propaganda.*
*Mishnah*, p. 189 (Babylon fire signals).
Pratkanis and Aronson. *Age of Propaganda.*
"Propaganda" in *Encyclopaedia Britannica.*
Rutherford. *Endless Propaganda.*

## Costly Signaling Theory

Irons. "Religion as a Hard to Fake Sign."
Sosis. "The Adaptive Value of Religious Ritual."

# 7

# Messages

I said earlier that when we communicate, the person (or animal, computer, etc.) who originates the communication expresses his or her thoughts as a message. The message is converted into a form that can be transmitted and the transmitted form is called a *signal*. The message is a representation of the thought the sender (if a human or thinking animal) has had and wants to create in the mind of the recipient. What does a message look or sound like? It can take many different forms. Suppose I want to express my feeling of the affection for someone. I want to say, "I love you." How can I do it?

# A Message as a Representation of a Thought

I know what I want the other person to understand. I know how I want the other person to feel. The problem is how to represent the message so as to best accomplish my objectives.

I can send it as English words. These can be recorded in handwriting or printing on paper and then mailed. I can convert the letters of my message into Morse code and send it by telegraph. I can send it in any of several ways as a series of carefully encoded gestures. If the other person and I can see each other, I may purse my lips to seem like kissing, or kiss my hand and seem to blow it toward the person. If we both know American Sign Language, I can "sign" my message, as in figure 7.1. If we're both sailors I can use semaphore flags. On and on. I can speak my message in French instead of English, or send a bouquet of flowers or a box of candy.

Figure 7.1. *Sending a message containing words, using hand symbols.* This is "I love you" in American Sign Language.

# How to Represent a Thought

Which method to use depends on several factors. What form of representation am I able to use? Do I know Morse code? What transmission channels are available? Is there pen and paper at hand? Is there a way to mail or deliver a written message? Do we both know the semaphore code? Are there semaphore flags available? Is it daytime? You can't see flags well in the dark. If I am speaking, whether in English or French, how will my words be transmitted? By sound waves? By telephone? If I'm sending flowers, can I find the right kind? Is there a way to deliver them?

Remember, I also talked about the importance of making sure the recipient understands the message, or gets the same meaning from it that the sender intended him or her to get. If you want to write in English can the recipient read it? Understand the English?

If you want to send Morse code, does the recipient have a telegraph receiver? Or is there a telegraph office nearby that can convert the coded message to written form and then deliver it?

Do you speak French? Does the recipient understand French? There are many different "natural languages" and the differences among them often cause difficulties in communicating (see box on following page). These are the languages we "naturally" speak and learn as children. Within a group that shares a common language, different from other groups, their language brings the members closer together, just as going to a particular school, belonging to a club or athletic team, or having served in an elite military organization creates a common feeling among the members or students.

Examples of non-natural, or artificial, languages are: the computer language BASIC, mathematics, sign language, or Esperanto. There are many sign languages—American Sign Language for the hearing impaired, the signs used by baseball umpires, those used by traffic police, those used by dogs. I once misinterpreted a dog's "clear" signal to me to rub his belly. Only that wasn't what he was saying, and I have the scar to prove it. Esperanto is like a natural language, but it did not evolve from the way people talked; it was consciously designed and perhaps for that reason never became widespread.

The closeness of people who share a language, hence also a culture, has been the cause of political battles over language in several countries that have more than one national language. In Canada, French-speaking people in Québec periodically try to declare independence from Canada. Americans have struggled with problems between citizens who speak Spanish over whether or not to permit Spanish as a language of instruction in school programs.

Belgium has had similar problems between citizens who speak French and those who speak Flemish (a variety of Dutch).

---

***Natural language and native speakers.*** Natural language is defined by one dictionary as "a language used natively by people, as opposed to an artificial language or code." So, what is a language used natively? It's the language we first learn in the home. Our parents use it, our siblings use it, our friends use it. It's natural in the sense that, well, naturally we speak the language of our parents and those we grow up with.

Noam Chomsky, professor of linguistics at MIT, proposed the theory that there is a universal grammar, that our brains are so constructed as to enable us to understand this kind of language, and that there are many variations called by such names as Greek, French, Swahili, and Hindi. That makes it very much "natural."

Most of us learn one language when we are small children. A few have parents each of whom speaks a different primary language. These children may grow up bilingual, that is knowing two languages really well. For the rest, we become what is called *native speakers* of that one language. We learn it from those around us. Even before we start school around the age of five, we can speak the language fairly well, although no one gave us formal lessons.

Only rarely do we learn the vocabulary, grammar, and pronunciation of new languages as well as we learned this first one. We know many rules of grammar and usage without consciously knowing that we do.

We don't have to be explicitly taught not to say, "My sister's birthday is tomorrow and we are having a party for him." And we learn quickly enough to say, "That book is mine," rather than, "That book is of me." For most of us, we will never know another language as well as we know our native language. That is why learners try to consult native speakers to explain some difficult usage point. What is really remarkable is how young we were when we learned it.

Do you want to send flowers? Most people like to get them, but what they mean is not always clear. Sometimes we send them just to be nice or to say thanks for a nice dinner. Should that be interpreted as "I love you"? Does the color of the flowers matter? Red roses are probably the most common way to "say it with flowers" when "it" is "I love you." But what about white roses? In France, the sending of white flowers is usually reserved for religious or solemn occasions such as funerals. They would not be the best way to gain romantic favor. You have to be careful when representing your thoughts through this kind of nonverbal symbol. Let us take a look at more ways to represent thoughts.

## Gesture

Can you tell the difference between the message in the left and right columns in figure 7.2?

There are languages of gesture for people who cannot hear. The native peoples of the American Plains tended to have a different natural language for each tribal group and it was rare that members of one group would learn the language of another. This clearly limited communication. However, they also recognized the importance of communication, so they developed a sign language or a language of gesture that was in common almost all Plains peoples from Canada to the Gulf of Mexico.[1] Dance is gesture, the antics of cheerleaders at a ballgame is gesture, as is saluting the flag as it passes in a parade, or rising when *The Star Spangled Banner* is played. We know that many varieties of animals can communicate information by gesture. They also make noises, and different noises have different meanings. Dogs, cats, monkeys, birds, and horses all do this. Bees communicate the location of a source of nectar by an elaborate dance performed before their hive mates.

Figure 7.2. *Sending nonverbal messages by gesture.* The meanings of these should be quite clear. Messages b and c appear similar in some ways, but look carefully at the faces and hands because they tell the story.

How did humans begin to communicate? We do not know exactly because no one was keeping records or writing history back then. But we do know that many animals can communicate information by gesture. People probably did so before they could speak in words and certainly before we had anything that we would call civilization.

**Voice**

You can say the words *Je t'aime* (I love you) in French. The poet Elizabeth Browning wrote, "How do I love thee? Let me count the ways." Then she went on to describe the ways. There is almost no limit to how our basic thoughts can be expressed in words. Since it evolved into a medium that made use of words, not merely grunts, the spoken word has become our primary means of communicating with other people.

## Drawing and Writing

This form of communication is quite old in our history. It was pointed out in Chapter 1 that archeologists had found drawings and carvings of images in European caves that are as much as 50,000 years old. Drawing and speech seemed to combine to evolve into writing. Writing is a way of representing spoken words by pictures or shapes.

## Music

Like flowers, the meaning of music can be ambiguous and some-times just plain baffling. Is there a musical passage you would use to mean "I love you"? Adding words to the music can make the meaning clearer so the message will have greater impact than the words alone or the music alone. But music by itself does have the capability to make a person feel good, even if not to make clear our love. William Congreve put it that, "Music hath charms to soothe the savage breast."[2] It can also arouse savage instincts, as in football, or some patriotic songs, sometimes without words. There is even a theory that a form of music came into use before human speech, but it really does not matter which came first. We now have both.

## Sculpture

Perhaps sculpting is not the best medium for sending our message, although some pieces of sculpture might do it, such as Rodin's famous statue *The Kiss*. Other sculptures can inspire reverence, as does Leonardo da Vinci's *Pieta*, or awe as does the statue of Abraham Lincoln in the Lincoln Memorial in Washington, D.C. (figure 7.3). Architecture can be thought of as a form of sculpture. Cathedrals are usually designed so that a person entering almost always looks up—toward heaven? And perhaps the person is also made to feel insignificant compared with the purpose of the cathedral. Many monuments or memorials send an intense emotional message to the viewer. The memorial to Vietnam War dead in Washington, shown in figure 7.4, is the most frequently visited such monument in Washington, which has relatively little visual appeal, but it lists the names of all members of the American forces who died in the war, giving it highly personal meaning to those whose relatives or friends died in the war. The Taj Mahal in India (figure 7.5) is a monument to a lost love. Seeing it is often a moving experience even for people with no direct involvement with the person who had it built or the loved one who died. My daughter, who took the picture, shed tears when she saw it, so moved was she by its beauty.

## Odor, Taste, and Touch

We can also express ourselves to some extent with our sense of *smell*. Flowers, in addition to their looks, have a pleasing aroma. There is perfume and the aroma of a favorite food. There's *texture*,

Figure 7.3. *Lincoln Memorial in Washington, D.C.* For some observers, Mr. Lincoln seems about to get up from his chair and come down to talk with them. Photo from U.S. National Park Service.

Figure 7.4. *Vietnam Memorial in Washington, D.C.* From any distance, this does not pack much of an emotional wallop, but up close, as visitors see the names of friends or relatives killed in the war, it is highly emotional. Photo courtesy of Alessandro della Valle.

Figure 7.5. *The Taj Mahal in Agra, India.* Like the previous two memorials, this was erected in memory of someone beloved who had died. It is considered by many to be the most beautiful building in the world. Photo by Sandra Meadow.

the smooth feel of satin or silk. There's *taste*. A gift of candy always seems to convey good feelings even to dieters. Caressing a person's hand sends quite a different signal from shaking hands. Cats and dogs use odor to send messages, as in figure 7.6, to other cats and dogs about who owns what piece of territory. They tend to record their marks on telephone poles and fire hydrants. Because of their superior (to us) senses of smell, they can read much information in this kind of message. A dog owner watching her own and other dogs walk around a park sniffing vigorously once said to me, "They're reading the news—who [which dogs] were here and what they had for dinner."

Figure 7.6. *Another way to send a message.* To humans this is meaningless and perhaps offensive. To other dogs, the message is quite clear, "I was here. This is my area."

## Messages Come through Our Senses

We modern humans have a wide range of means by which we can represent thought and send messages. We have our five senses to be used for receiving signals: seeing, hearing, touching or feeling, tasting, and smelling. We can send messages to be received using any of one these or a combination. Other animals do, too. But humans have the ability, far superior to dogs or any other animals, to make different sounds and interpret the meanings of those sounds. On the other hand, dogs and other animals can detect and interpret odors that we cannot detect and often see better in the dark than we can.

Helen Keller lived from 1880 to 1968. At eighteen months of age she became ill and as a result lost the ability to hear and see. Think about that. Most humans receive most of their messages with these two senses. We hear and understand speech and we learn to speak long before we can read or write. At the age of seven Miss Keller learned to receive messages mostly by feel, having her teacher trace letters on her hand. She had to learn that these letters combined into words and that words described things. In spite of her handicaps, she was able to graduate from Radcliffe College at age 24 and went on to a distinguished career as writer and lecturer. This was a remarkable feat that demonstrates how we can use different trans-mission media to get any given message across.

"A large variety of animals possess a magnetic sense. Migratory birds use magnetic clues (in addition to light polarization, star signs, position of the sun) to find their way south in fall and north in spring. Salamanders [and] frogs use the magnetic field for orientation when they have to find the direction of the nearest shore quickly, e.g., when they sense danger."[3] These animals, all with brains very much smaller than those of humans are able to directly sense a magnetic field. Such signals (existence and orientation of the field) are not sent for the purpose of guiding the birds, but they use the signals in somewhat the same way that we do. We use instruments—compasses—to detect the magnetic field of the earth, which enables us to find our way through oceans and forests.

Bees and butterflies can see ultraviolet light. You probably know that your TV remote communicates with the receiver set by use of infrared light, which we humans cannot see. Ultraviolet is at the other end of the visible color spectrum (see box on next page). It's the kind of "light" (is it light if we can't see it?) that can cause damage to our eyes or our skin by too much exposure. The bees and butterflies use it to see some flowers that emit this kind of light.

The point of all this is that communicating using combinations of speech, music, drawing and writing, gesture, odor, touch, or taste gives humans a very powerful way to send messages, powerful in the sense that we can convey so many different meanings with very subtle variations. And we can get our point across in different ways:

touch instead of speech, odor instead of taste, music instead of writing. Some creatures on this earth can use different senses than we have.

## The Medium and the Message

Marshall McLuhan, one of the great theorists about communication in the late 20th century, as noted in chapter 5, used the phrase "the medium is the message," now often quoted. Originally, he had used the phrase "The medium is the *massage*" as the title of a book, but later changed *massage* to *message*. But what exactly does it mean? It doesn't mean that if you know the medium used, say writing, speaking, or televising, you would know the content of any message sent. But it does mean that the medium used to represent or transmit your message can make a big difference in how the recipient understands or reacts to your message. What's the best way to get people interested in buying your brand of automobile? It could be by

*Light spectrum.* All light is part of a larger phenomenon called the electromagnetic spectrum. Electromagnetic waves include, in addition to visible light, X-rays, radio waves, and cosmic rays. By visible light we mean that portion of the spectrum that we humans can sense with our eyes. Normally, we think of there being seven colors: violet, indigo, blue, green, yellow, orange, and red. There is no fixed boundary between what is red and what is orange. Certain colors are seen by one person as a shade of yellow, another as a shade of orange. There are also forms of light we cannot see: infrared and ultraviolet. We don't see ultraviolet, but it tans or burns our skin. We can't see infrared, but we use it in our TV remote units to carry our signals to the receiver.

What's the difference among the waves, that is, what makes orange or green? It's the wave frequency. Red has the lowest frequency and longest waves of all visible light. Violet is the opposite, highest frequency, shortest waves. Infrared means "below red"; ultraviolet means "beyond violet."

putting a printed, black and white ad in a newspaper with full technical specifications but no pictures. Or the ad could be on color television showing a person driving the car through beautiful scenery accompanied by the man or woman of dreams. We all know which mode gets the most advertising dollars.

Whether a newspaper, magazine, or radio or television program, each is a different medium and each carries content to its destinations. What exactly do the media sell to the advertiser? They are not really selling content; that is what they sell to the viewers. To the advertiser they are selling the *attention* of the person at the destination. Yes, they rely on content of scheduled programs or news or features to attract recipient attention, but they do not emphasize to the advertiser how true the stories are or how entertaining, they tell how many readers' attention they capture and that number, as well as description of the readers or viewers, is what sells. Buyers of advertising on the mass media spend a great deal of money and do a great deal of research to guide their buying decisions.

William Shakespeare wrote the play *Romeo and Juliet* around 1594. It was about two young people in love who came from families continually feuding with each other. The result was misunderstanding and tragedy when both lovers died. Leonard Bernstein in 1957 produced a similar play, *West Side Story*, set to music. This time it was about two young people in New York each connected with a different feuding street gang. The two fell in love and then they, like Romeo and Juliet, came to tragic ends. Which attracts a modern audience more, particularly of young people— acting plus modern music or Shakespearean English? This is not to denigrate Shakespeare but to point out that modern young people who have not been exposed much to the classics of English literature but do know about street gangs might take to Bernstein more readily than to Shakespeare.

Many people never read newspapers. What news they get comes from television, where they see live pictures of the story but get less detail. Which attracts the larger audience? Which provides the most information?

McLuhan was right. The medium we choose to send a message greatly affects the way that message will be received and paid attention to. Is that why the advertising industry has become so important in modern life? Not just to sell products but also to "sell" politicians and even religion.

---

I have shown that the message is the thing communicated and the signal is a form of the message that fits the selected mode of transmission. Of critical importance are both assuring that the message correctly represents the thought of the sender and is likely to result in desired understanding by the recipient.

Humans have a great variety of means of communication available to us which enables us to enrich our lives by enjoying messages received by any or all of our senses, by being able to send messages in so many forms, and by allowing us to recover from loss or impairment of any sense.

# Notes

1. von Frisch, *The Dance Language and Orientation of Bees*.
2. William Congreve, *The Mourning Bride*.
3. Ritz and Schulten, "The Magnetic Sense of Animals" (Web site).

# Further Reading

## Natural Language

Bodmer. *The Loom of Language*.
Chomsky. *On Natural Language*.
———. *On Nature and Language*.
———. *Knowledge of Language*.
"Language" in *Encyclopaedia Britannica*.
Pinker. *The Language Instinct*.
Yule. *The Study of Language*.

## Nonverbal Communication

"Animal communication" in *Encyclopaedia Britannica*.
Hall. *The Silent Language*.
Morris. *Body Talk*.
Morris et al. *Gestures, Their Origins and Distribution*.
Sebeok. *How Animals Communicate*.

## Senses, Human and Animal

Geldard, *The Human Senses*.
Pollan. *The Botany of Desire*. (Communication from plants.)
Smith. *Biology of Sensory Systems*.
Articles from *Encyclopaedia Britannica:*
    "Insect: Sensory Perception and Receptors"
    "Sensory Receptors, Human"
    "The Nervous System and Sensory Organs"

*The following articles are from scientific journals and may be difficult reading:*
    Ritz, Adem, and Schulten. "A Model for Photoreceptor-Based Magneto-reception in Birds." *Biophysical Journal* 78 (2000), pp. 707–18.
    Walker, Denis, and Kirschvink. "The Magnetic Sense and Its Use in Long-Distance Navigation by Animals." *Current Opinion in Neurobiology*, 12 (6), Dec. 2002, pp. 735–44.

## Messages as Representations of Thought

Coren. *How to Speak Dog*.
Nieh. "Stingless-Bee Communication."
McLuhan. *Understanding Media*.
Meadow et al. *Text Information, Retrieval Systems*, pp. 49–67.
Penzias. *Ideas and Information*, pp. 38–66.
von Frisch. *The Dance Language and Orientation of Bees*.

# 8

# Signs and Symbols

Remember that human communication means sending a thought from an originator to a recipient and that the communication goes from the mind of one person to the mind of another. In order to do that the thought has to be formulated as a message and that message may be converted to a form that can be transmitted whether by sound, sight, electronics, writing, printing, or any other means. If sent by electronics, the message may be transformed several times. In each of its forms, the message must be represented by a series of symbols.

# The Idea of a Symbol

One formal definition of a symbol or sign is "something which stands to somebody for something in some respect or capacity."[1] That was surely intended as a sort of serious joke when it was written in 1897, but it can be a serious definition. A symbol is "something." It can be almost anything that a human or animal or even a machine working on behalf of a human can see, hear, feel, taste, smell, or otherwise detect. It doesn't have to be anything special, as long as it is different from most other symbols. The period at the end of this sentence is a symbol. So is the space after the period. Why only different from "most other symbols"? See the section on "Value of Ambiguity" on p. 153.

A symbol must stand for something "to somebody." A symbol doesn't have meaning by nature and for *everyone*, but it has to mean something to *someone*. Actually, it ought to mean the same thing to at least two people.

It has to stand "for something." Well, yes; symbols are part of a message that tells something. If the symbol does not stand for anything, it can't be telling anything.

Finally, it stands for something to somebody "in some respect or capacity." It does not have to have the same meaning all the time. The symbol "St." can mean either *saint* or *street*. It's rare that the meanings would be confused. 123 St. James St. is not ambiguous to native speakers of English. The saint meaning would be followed by a person's name. The street meaning would come after a name or number and be in the context of describing a place or route to some place.

To summarize, a symbol has to be something recognizable; it has to mean something to someone, but it may have different meanings in different circumstances. Let's consider some examples. Symbols are most useful when they have the same meaning among a group of people. The words of a language, a secret handshake for members of a club, or a bugle call only have to have meaning to limited groups of people.

# Examples

As we said earlier, one of the earliest forms of writing, or really what led to writing, was using various clay shapes to represent objects, mainly items bought or sold in trade. These eventually evolved into pictures of the objects and eventually into writing as we know it. But the clay shapes did their job in a day when it was the only way to record a representation of concepts or things and when the symbol had to be preserved and moved from place to place, as from the buyer on credit to the seller. Three-dimensional symbols are harder to store or to move than those on a flat surface, but they are still used today. A bald eagle is a symbol of the United States, not just a two-dimensional picture of an eagle, but the three-dimensional, living bird itself. A red, white, and blue striped pole is a symbol indicating that behind it is a barber shop. This symbol is hundreds of years old. The Inuit people of the Arctic region use a symbol called an *inuksuk* (see figure 8.1) to send a variety of messages. In the Inuit language it means *to act in place of a human*. In other words, it sends a message to a person walking near it that a human might have sent, if present. It can indicate direction of a path, location of a food source, or any of many other possible meanings. It consists of rocks piled up in a meaningful pattern. There is no fixed dictionary of meaning to the various parts and it is not secret, but, generally, only a member of the culture can understand it.

Figure 8.1. *An Inuit inuksuk, message to travelers.* These Inuit (peoples of the Canadian and Greenland arctic) structures can have different meanings, but in general they would be placed along a trail to provide information for a traveler such as the direction to take along the trail or the location of a food source. Photo courtesy of Judith Varney Burch Gallery creation of the inuksuk by Norman Hallendy.

A gesture by a person or animal is not recorded, but the gesture is a symbol and it means something. I showed some human gestures in figure 7.2. Figure 8.2 shows a traffic sign commonly seen on North American roads when there is danger of fires in forests or fields. This one appeared in an Iranian newspaper whose language was Farsi. The point is that symbols like this are becoming universal because as people travel more and more there is need for signs giving directions in a form that almost anyone can recognize. A sign saying "No Smoking," in any written language, would not do the job.

Figure 8.2. *An Iranian traffic sign.* This will be familiar to North Americans, but it was taken from an Iranian newspaper, which indicates how widespread such symbols have become. It means "No smoking." Why a traffic symbol? Because anyone seeing this is probably traveling through an environmentally sensitive area.

An interesting animal gesture is used by most dogs, particularly young ones. Some background first: Dogs are descended from wolves. Both are pack animals—they like to live in groups with strong attachment to the group by its members. Status within the group is very important. There is always a leader, normally a male, called by humans the alpha dog. He gets his position by fighting for it. Lesser dogs in the pack may fight for status below the leader or may challenge to become leader. Puppies like to play, and their main game is a sort of wrestling. When one dog wants to play with another it makes a gesture called the *play bow*. The forelegs are flat on the ground, the hind legs are standing upright, and the tail is wagging as in figure 8.3. This means, "Let's play," and it implies, "We won't hurt each other." Some people who study animal behavior think it also says, "Whatever happens in this play fight will not affect our relative status in the pack. I'll still be number three and you'll be two regardless of what happens."

Figure 8.3. *A dog's play bow*. Just about a universal, inbred symbol for dogs, this is an invitation to play not too roughly. Find a dog under the age of one year and you will see this often, but it is also used by some older dogs who are still frisky.

Now, that's a pretty complex symbol. Dogs are smart creatures, but there is a limit. When two boys fight, even if they do not want to hurt each other, they probably both realize that if there is a clear winner, that boy gains recognition in the eyes of other boys who are watching. So, when two dogs play fight, they both have to understand the rule and any other dogs watching also have to understand what the symbol of the play bow meant and that the status of the combatants will not change. This symbol seems to be so important that it is inborn in dogs.[2]

Also remember that two-dimensional images including letters, words, numbers, and trademarks are symbols. The earliest actual writing was based on pictures standing for concepts of things, maybe a donkey or a house. There would have been a spoken word for each picture. Even in these purely pictorial writing systems, the images did not necessarily look like the thing symbolized. They were just symbols that differed from other symbols and that were learned by their users.

Although the original idea of an alphabet was that a single letter would represent a single sound, it is common that sometimes a letter can have more than one sound or even none (the *g* in *goal, geometry,* and *sign,* for example). So, we have a violation of our rules that a symbol has to have the same meaning for a group of people who use it. Many speakers of English, including native speakers, have trouble with words ending in *gh.* When is this silent and when pronounced like *f*? Is it as in *through* ("throo") or *tough* ("tuff")? We learn this by memorization. But what happens when we see a new word, say a name like Hough? Is that pronounced like *How, Hoo, Hue,* or *Huff*? What we have is ambiguity. It just is not clear what to do. There is more than one reasonable possibility for correct pronunciation. Our symbol system is not perfect and some misunderstandings can occur even among people who speak the language as natives. English, because it is made up from several different language groups, is maddeningly imperfect. We must all learn the meaning of a basic symbol, then other interpretations of it. and maybe how to tell which interpretation to use.

Even machines use symbols to communicate with each other. A fax machine instructed to send a message listens for a dial tone, which is a message from a telephone company machine to a caller. When the tone is heard the sending fax sends out symbols for the phone number of the intended recipient's fax machine. It follows this with a high-pitched tone, going out before the call is answered at the receiving end. The receiver's fax can sense this tone before it answers and it responds with a coded message stating its characteristics for receiving a transmission. Without that tone, the fax machine remains idle. Thus, if a fax and a voice telephone share a line, the fax can grab an incoming fax call first before the telephone user hears a ring (but not in older faxes). If it does not sense the high tone, the phone rings and a person or answering machine responds with a voice message.[3]

# Combining Basic Symbols into Words and Numbers

The alphabet, a simpler basic set of symbols than pictorial writing, works only because we can combine the basic symbols into other, larger symbols—letters combined into words. In addition to the pronunciation ambiguity mentioned earlier, there can be ambiguity in meaning because sometimes one string of letters can have more than one meaning, or two different strings of letters can have the same meaning. When two different words mean the same thing we call them *synonyms* from Greek words meaning *name* and *together*. When the same string of letters has more than one meaning we call the multiple meanings *homonyms*, or in Greek, same name. Once again, this means that among a group of people who communicate with each other, there has to be common understanding about word meanings or some way to decide which meaning is intended and there has to be understanding that more than one meaning can be understood by a recipient. The words *lead* and *lead* look alike, but one is a verb meaning to show the way or take charge, while the other is a noun indicating a kind of metal. To complicate things, the verb can be used as a noun, as to be in the lead, and the noun can be used as a verb, as to lead a stained glass window. The recipient of a message using one of these words must have some basis for deciding what meaning was intended. The knowledge base is called upon to help make this decision.

Putting a string of numerals together such as 123, as we know, means far more than that three symbols came together. The syntax is very precise (see chapter 1, p. 14).

There is a grammar in writing mathematical symbols and chemical symbols. Normally, to indicate adding two numbers together, we write $a + b$. There is another kind of notation some-times used in computer programming in which the sum of two numbers is indicated by $a, b, +$. If the writer and the reader both know that method called Polish notation, it's perfectly clear. If not, it's meaningless. The symbol 12 is a number and could be the number of anything. The symbol $12 makes it clear what 12 is the number of. It doesn't tell what $12 is the price of, but it does tell the number of dollars involved. A musical symbol can indicate a one-eighth note, as in figure 8.4a. Add a dot to the right of it, (b) and it says hold the note for the usual time plus half that time again. Put the dot in front of the note, (c) and it's simply a mistake.

a    b    c

Figure 8.4 *Symbols and syntax in music.* The single symbol at a is meaningful to a musician—an eighth note. The combined symbols at b tell a performer to hold the note for half again as long as the basic symbol indicates. The two symbols at c in the order presented mean nothing.

## Combining Word Symbols—Grammar

The next level of combining symbols is grammar or syntax. We can take the word *red* and the word *book* and make the phrase *red book*. We can make complete sentences: *Weijing read the red book.* To most speakers of English who hear this spoken, the occurrence of two words that sound alike, *read* and *red*, will not be a problem. Grammatical rules enable us to make complex statements and help us avoid ambiguity.

Modern English is very tolerant of grammatical errors, even if teachers and editors are not. The sentence "Everyone should bring their books to school" is technically not correct because *everyone* is singular and *their* is plural. The sentence "I ain't got no books" is wrong on two counts—it uses the no-no word *ain't* and uses a double negative, which, technically, means the speaker *does* have books. But most people would understand it as the speaker denying having any books. However, "I gave my sister the book and he lost it" leaves us scratching ours heads (a gestural symbol meaning "I do not understand"). If the book went to a sister, the speaker should have said *she*. Or did the speaker mean *brother*? We can't tell. A mistake like this is common among native speakers of a language that does not use gender-based pronouns. There will be more about understanding messages in chapter 10.

## The Value of Ambiguity

It can be frustrating for a person whose first language is not English to hear a sentence like "How is it going?" The response might be, "How is what going?" The English speaker who hears that response is equally puzzled because he or she expected to hear something like, "Fine, how about you?" It reminds us of the ambiguities so easily possible in English and very likely every other natural language. *Comment ça va?* (French for "How is it going?") can give a person not familiar with colloquial French the same problem. The other side of this coin is the power of our rather flexible syntax and lexical definitions of words. Without the ability to have our words and syntax take on meanings different from what we conventionally expect, we could have no or little poetry, and novelists, dramatists, and orators would have a difficult time being highly expressive. Even crossword puzzles would be affected since for they rely on ambiguity of the clues allowing more than one interpretation to befuddle the solver. In poetry and often in prose, there is no limit to the use of similes and metaphors. The whole point is to create an image in the reader's mind or to see a connection between two entities not previously recognized. A language so well defined as to have only one meaning per word, one word per meaning, and syntax so well defined that there is only one way to combine words into phrases would be not only dull but ineffective in communicating new ideas.

---

We have seen that symbols are what carry information whether in writing, speech, electric current, sculpture, or even odor. Consider the skunk: an intentional release of a certain odor means "Stay away." Symbols are not information—they stand for information provided that the person receiving the symbol understands what it was intended to signify. We have no other way to transfer meaning from one entity to another, be it human, animal, or machine, except by use of mutually understood symbols.

Symbols are not restricted to obvious shapes or sounds. They may be subtle gestures or written words—literature—that only hint at the author's meaning. We must sometimes struggle to find the appropriate symbols to use to express our meaning and, even more of a struggle, to figure out what someone else's symbols mean.

# Notes

1. Sebeok, *Signs*, p. 11.
2. Desmond Morris, personal communication to C. Meadow.
3. "Fax Technology—Testing Issues" (Web site).

# Further Reading

## Symbols

Chandler. *Semiotics: The Basics.*
———. "Semiotics for Beginners" (Web site).
Corballis. *From Hand to Mouth.*
Coren. *How to Speak Dog.*
Hayakawa and Hayakawa. *Language in Thought and Action.*
Schmandt-Besserat. *How Writing Came About.*
Sebeok. *Signs.*
von Frisch. *The Dance Language and Orientation of Bees.*

## Words and Numbers

Daniels and Daniels. *English Grammar.*
Ifrah. *From One to Zero.*
Pinker. *Words and Rules.*
Yule. *The Study of Language.*

# 9

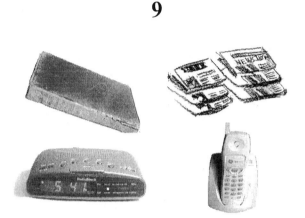

# Media and Transmission

In chapter 5 we pointed out that *medium* is a word that means, or originally meant, middle or something in the middle. A recording medium is something on which we can record a message, whether the message is a picture, sound, words, or even an odor. Today, newspapers and radio and television broadcasters are individually and collectively referred to as *the media*. These are organizations that distribute information or play a role between the event they report and the people who see, hear, or read about it. The telephone is a medium of transmission. It carries messages from here to there, hence, is in the middle between a message originator and its destination.

*Content* refers to the essence of a message—what it says or means—whether it consists of words, pictures, or stage or television plays. It is important to be aware of the difference between the medium that delivers messages, the content of the messages, and the effect of the medium on the recipient's reaction to the content.

# Types of Media

Let's review the types of media in more detail. Basically, there are three broad types in communications:

> *Organizations* that collect information (content) and distribute it (radio stations, the post office),
>
> *Recordings* or *substances* upon which messages are recorded (stone, paper, magnetic disks, photographic film), and
>
> *Channels* or *carriers* (sound waves, electromagnetic waves).

We'll begin with the organizations that produce content.

## Media as Organizations

The telegraph, which has by now almost disappeared from the world's scene, and the telephone, almost as old but still going strong, are mostly transmission media that carry messages from point to point or person to person. Newspapers, magazines, books, radio and television, and motion pictures are called *mass media*. They are intended to reach a large audience at one time with the same message. It takes a rather large organization to produce the content of the mass media. Examples are the staffs of CNN, *The Washington Post*, and SONY Music.

In point-to-point communication, one person or source communicates with one other at any given time. Telephone and postal service are examples. In most countries telephone and postal organizations are very large, but any given message usually goes to only one recipient, although there is junk mail, magazines and so forth sent to multiple addressees, in which case the mail becomes a mass medium. Telephone allows for conference calls involving three or more participants. Both types of media started as point-to-point channels.

Newspapers, collectively, are called *the press*. Whether major national dailies such as *The Los Angeles Times,* a neighborhood weekly, or the newsletter of a small organization, they serve pretty much the same function. They collect news, announcements such as advertisements, editorial and opinion pieces, and entertainments such as comics and crossword puzzles. They may do this by sending reporters out to the scene of some activity or receiving stories and features written by someone not on their staff, such as the Associated Press or authors of letters to the editor. They have editors who must decide which stories to print and who may change the content to correct grammatical or spelling errors or to shorten a story. They add headlines to attract readers' attention.

Before the invention of radio, newspapers or letters were just about the only means by which an average reader could know what was happening in the world outside his or her own community. Therefore, the paper's or letter writer's choice of what to write about and what slant or bias to take affected what readers thought about the subject. Newspapers often represent particular political interests, so they may be known as Democratic or Republican papers or liberal or conservative. Not all bias is bad. It may be a bias in favor of true reporting and away from spreading rumor, or repeating press releases from governments or companies as truth. An expression such as "I read it in the paper"or "I read it in the *Times*" was commonly used and still is to some extent today. Such expressions tell of the speaker's belief in the reliability of the source.

Book publishers play a similar role, but instead of publishing as quickly as possible after an event, they must wait until a book about the event is written and this can be many years after the event. So, books are not generally a news medium, but they do provide background and understanding about news and people in the news and, of course, they tell stories and present educational material. Book publishers also have editors who select what is to be published and sometimes change the content for such reasons as to improve syntax or readability or to avoid libel or copyright infringement. Book publishers are less likely to have a corporate point of view on content, although they may. Books sell to consumers only after they are published, unlike newspapers. Books do not tend to rely on today's stories to sell an issue.

Radio can mean an organization, teams of people with equipment who produce programs, and networks of individual producers. Radio is also a means of transmission that is quite independent of who created the program to be transmitted. It was the first mass medium that brought its messages directly into the home as it was being sent. It led to the family and friends gathering around the set—the receiver—and listening to favorite programs. News could have been sent earlier by telephone but only to one destination at a time. Radio created the mass audience. In chapter 4 I mentioned a rare and short-lived way to broadcast news, and music that used the telephone in late 19th-century Budapest, Hungary. Like the press, radio could be influential because of the information it chose to transmit and the slant or bias it may have introduced into its content. "I read it in the paper" often became "I heard it on the radio."

In some ways, television is not much different from radio. They require the same kind of organization to create and distribute content. But television content is more expensive to produce and, because it shows pictures, has the ability to hold an average viewer's attention more than radio—if done well. But the attention may be short lived. One of the criticisms of TV, of its news programs, its dramatic programs, and political advertising is that it is all too short. We tend to get news headlines, not much deep news analysis, and dramatic programs that create and solve problems in twenty-two minutes of the scheduled half-hour show. During an election campaign we get thirty-second "sound bites" in which a candidate says a few nice-sounding words, often promising more spending and less taxation but no explanation of how they can both be done. There can be little question, though, that television has captured the attention of huge audiences, something never before done by any medium. Broadcasts, particularly of sports events such as the Super Bowl, Olympics, or World Cup of Soccer, draw worldwide audiences in hundreds of millions of people.

Motion pictures and the companies that make and distribute them are both media. Making a motion picture is much like making a television program but usually far more expensive. In other ways movies are similar to books in that they must be produced before they are sold to consumers. They can have a great influence on how people think, for good or bad. Often criticized for having too much sex and violence, they are also capable of bringing sensitive issues to the screen and helping viewers understand people who are different from themselves. It can be a medium of great emotional power.

## Recording Media

Let's be clear on the difference between a recording medium and a transmission medium. Recording means to put a message onto some medium from which it can be read, seen, heard, felt, or smelled at a later time. You are now reading a book whose words were printed on paper some time ago so that you could read them at your convenience at a future time. A musical recording is similar. It is usually recorded in a studio to be heard by the intended audience at some future time. A fine silk fabric is made in a factory so that someone later can feel its smoothness and appreciate its colors. Statues and words are carved into stone to be viewed many years later. Photography records images on glass, film, or paper. We even get magazines that have scratch-and-smell pieces. After removal of an outer layer, an odor comes through, usually to sell perfume or some other cosmetic product. Transmission, on the other hand, moves a message, however recorded. Not all transmission systems are instantaneous or even rapid. The message can be moved through space, time, or both. Carrying the mail on horseback across a continent is a transmission system that clearly takes a long time to deliver its message, but telephone, radio, and television are virtually instantaneous. Transmission systems are not usually concerned with recording messages except as necessary to transmit them, not to save them.

Specifically, the major recording media in use today are paper, computer disks and tape, musical disks and tape, television disks

(DVD) and tape (VHS), and the many substances on which a painting can be put. The various kinds of disks and tapes for recording computer data, sounds, and video images are becoming more and more the same as these others. They can be "read" by computers, stereos, or televisions. Remember, though, that these media record, they do not transmit. A computer's central processor, but not the disks, can send signals to the telephone or cable systems for transmission. The coming together of different recording or transmitting methods is called *convergence* of media, and we shall see more and more of it until, possibly, these three types of media and readers all merge into a single recording form and a single machine for reading.

Paper comes in a great variety of forms for different uses. At one extreme are sanitary papers, used for handkerchiefs, paper napkins, towels, and general wiping. At the other extreme are fine papers used for formal documents such as diplomas, postage stamps, or money or for recording of photographic images. In between are book papers, newsprint (a less expensive and shorter-lived paper than is used for books), and office papers used for computer output and letters. One of the curiosities of the modern world is that the huge increase in electronic and magnetic record-ings has brought with them a huge increase in the use of this last category of paper. Many people, happy to transmit or receive letters or longer documents via the computer, insist on printing them before reading them.[1]

Remember, also, that the word *medium* may be applied to the tool used for recording as well as the substance upon which a signal is recorded. Examples are pens, printers, computer disk drives (rather than the disks themselves), and cameras. There may be some debate as to whether electromagnetic waves are a substance, but I'll skip that argument.

## Signal-Carrying Media

Sound and light carry symbols, and they have been used since time beyond recall to carry the sounds of a voice or the sight of a gesture. Both, in their raw state, are limited in range. The sound of a human or animal voice typically may go for a few hundred meters, the actual distance depending on the frequency of the sound and the environment—heavy forest, open prairie or desert, high alps. Light is almost unlimited. We can see stars many light years away (1 light-year = 9.4 trillion km or 5.9 trillion miles). But on the surface of the earth we are limited by trees and hills and the sharpness of the human eye.

Wires and cables are relatively new as signal carriers—used only since the middle of the 19th century. The ultimate in current technology is the fiber optic cable. This is actually a thin glass fiber. The signal is sent as variations in the intensity of a light beam sent through this fiber. The capacity challenges the comprehension of most nontechnical people. It carries far more than any of us wants, but it is highly reliable and can handle more than one simultaneous transmission. This is the technology that fed the spurt in telecommunications company shares in the late 1990s and early years of the 21st century. Fiber optic cables are replacing heavy, expensive telephone and television cables both over land and under the sea.

## Transmission Systems

Transmission media receive messages or symbolic representations of messages and convert them into signals to be sent out through a channel or carrier. Transmission media do not produce the content of clients' messages, exercise editorial selection over what to transmit, or editorially modify the messages. Nor do they record for posterity; they just send.

Transmission systems may take part in preparing the message for sending whether by wire or electromagnetic waves, sound, mail, or other modes; carrying the message through a channel; or even carrying the messenger. Typically, transmission requires an organization to arrange for reception of the original message, as well as the machinery to actually enter it into (or onto) the carrier. Our telephone companies best typify this form of medium.

We have not given up the old methods yet. We may have given up the Pony Express, but only the horse, not the mail courier. The post office and the private courier companies are also transmission media. They do not publish what they distribute except for zip code directories or the like. But they carry a great deal of content originated by others. They are not supposed to exercise any control over what is sent unless there is a violation of the law involved. They can't decide that they only want to deliver mail that tells about foreign affairs or baseball. They take it all. Today, our mail boxes are filled daily with paper mail, mostly advertising, and our streets with FedEx, Purolator, UPS, and other trucks and the ubiquitous bicycle couriers. Bicycle couriers, almost paradoxically, thrive in crowded cities, usually the sites of the highest of hi-tech equipment. But, the big cities are often traffic-bound and a bike can maneuver more easily than a car or truck. Several big city police departments have also discovered this phenomenon and have some bicycle-mounted patrol officers.

In a telegraph office, messages were usually delivered to it by the sender, converted to code in the mind of the operator, then sent out over a wire. For the electronic media, transmission is mostly done by machines. A camera or microphone picks up images or sounds, they are converted for transmission and sent by wire, cable, or electromagnetic waves.

## Media, Hot and Cold

Marshall McLuhan had a new way of looking at media. He called a medium *cool* if it gave only low definition (it required the viewer's mind to fill in some of the imagery). The recipient must add to the received message by imagining scenery, facial expressions, and actions mentioned but not depicted. The standard telephone, for example, cannot present pictures. The listener at one end cannot see the speaker at the other and cannot be sure what that person is feeling. Radio can do better. Even though it does not show pictures, it is written and acted to get the listener to envision a scene. A *hot* medium grabs the viewer's attention and holds it, showing explicitly what it wants the user to imagine. Motion pictures do this or can do it if well written, acted, and photographed. McLuhan thought of television as cool, but it has improved technologically and in terms of the quality of programs sometimes found since McLuhan's day.

This classification is not perfect because it is so dependent on how the messages are presented. Modern high-definition television is capable of much more definition than 1960s black and white or early color presented on small screens and with writing and acting not up to what was seen in movies or on the stage. Also, different people will react differently to media.

# Noise

In everyday language, noise means an unpleasant or loud sound. But in communications it has a more exact meaning and has nothing to do with esthetics. Noise is an addition to a signal that was not intended by the originator. The most obvious example is the noise we call static on a radio or telephone. Static is unpleasant and, even more, it interferes with reception. The destination may not receive the message that was intended because of the noise. Sometimes, especially in war time, one nation's radio or radar transmissions have been effectively blocked by another country sending out massive amounts of noise on the same frequency.

In figure 9.1 I show a revision of the Shannon diagram first presented in chapter 5. This is the way he originally presented it, showing noise being input to the communications channel. We cannot know all the sources of noise in general, but we know that it is ever present to some degree and that steps are always needed to try to block it out.

If the transmission system is electric, like the telephone, noise can be caused by a thunderstorm that alters the flow of electricity through cables. It can even be caused by a squirrel nibbling away

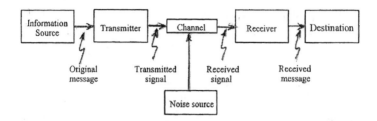

Figure 9.1. *Shannon diagram showing presence of noise.* This is more like Shannon's original diagram, showing noise entering the communication system through the channel which changes the form of the received message.

at the insulation covering the cables, thereby exposing the bare metal to various form of electromagnetic noise in the air. Of course, if transmission is by electromagnetic waves traveling through the air, noise can be added to the intended waves. These can come from, again, thunderstorms or the sun or other celestial bodies, automobile engines, or virtually any electronic equipment. Radio receivers emit a small amount of radio waves as well as receive them. Computers are also emitters of unwanted radiation. That is why you are asked not to use portable radios, cell phones, or computers on airplanes at certain times during a flight.

Television noise can appear as static but also as various distortions in the visual image. The most common of these is "snow," the appearance of white flecks on the screen that look like a heavy snow fall. There can also be ghost images, which can be caused by reflection of a signal off an obstacle such as a tall building or mountain in effect sending the same signal to you twice or more, but each extra one is set off in time, and in distance when displayed, by just enough to be annoying. This was shown in figure 5.5. Cable television was originally developed both to counter these noise generators and to pull in signals from far away. The use of cable has mostly eliminated these problems.

When a document, newspaper, or old letter ages, the paper turns yellow or brown, the ink may fade, and acid or tiny creatures may eat away at the paper. These conditions can make reading the text difficult and cause errors in getting the message as in figure 9.2. Hence, flaking or discoloration of paper or fading of ink are forms of noise in the world of printing. It's even possible to think of poor grammar or phrasing in natural language as a source of noise because they are unintended and may interfere with the recipient getting the message that was intended. This is very common when speaking in a foreign language with which we have a low degree of competence.

The detection and elimination of noise is a large part of what communication engineers do. For those of us who send and receive messages but do not design transmission systems, we must at least be aware that noise could interfere or might have interfered with a signal. Then we must consider what to do. Did the message get correctly converted to a signal? How do we know? Did the recipient get the message we sent? How do we know?

How do we combat noise? There are two basic ways, *shielding* and *redundancy*. Shielding means putting up a barrier to the noise. Perhaps the simplest example is putting a hand over one ear when talking on the telephone in a noisy room. That shuts out some of the sounds we don't want to hear. More elaborate shielding could involve sound deadening paneling in a room. Also there are forms of electromagnetic shielding. The telephone cables we see on the

Figure 9.2. *Noise in printed matter*. This is a segment of the Dead Sea Scrolls, showing parts of the page missing (taking away part of the signal is a form of noise), part obscured by what could be decay, water, or insect damage.

street are shielded by a coating of nonelectrically conducting (but squirrel attracting at times) material. Coaxial cable, the kind used to bring the television cable from the wall to our receiver, consists of a wire of the conventional kind surrounded by some insulation, which is in turn surrounded by a metal sheath that bars unwanted electromagnetic waves from getting to the signal-carrying wire. The whole is encased in another layer of insulation as shown in figure 9.3.

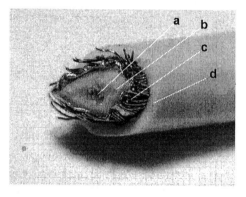

Figure 9.3. *A coaxial cable.* A coaxial cable consists of a conventional wire (a) surrounded by insulation (b) to prevent or reduce entry of electromagnetic radiation in the atmosphere from entering the wire, and a metal covering (c), which also protects against radiation as well as physical damage, for example, by mice or squirrels. Finally, the whole is wrapped in a waterproof insulation material (d). Some noise may still get through, but far less than for conventional electric wires. Photo by the author.

Say you're in a crowded, noisy restaurant having trouble hearing the people at your table talk and having them hear you. How do you get your message across? Usually in such circumstances we talk louder and slower and enunciate carefully. These are forms of *redundancy*, in effect sending extra signals so that if some parts are lost, enough of the message gets through to accomplish the goal.

Redundancy is something the sender of a message needs to be aware of, perhaps to consciously build into a message to ensure its proper receipt. Talking louder raises the level of the signal compared with the noise or increases the signal-to-noise ratio, as in figure 9.4. (But, of course, when traveling in a foreign country, shouting louder in English to a person who doesn't understand you does not help. The problem there is not noise, it is lack of recognition of meaning.)

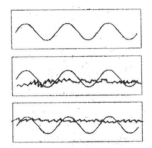

Figure 9.4. *Signal-to-noise ratio*. The top graph represents a simple signal, something like a warbling emergency siren. There is no noise. The next graph shows the same signal with a fairly low level of noise—a level that might bother a listener of music but not one listening to a siren. The bottom graph shows a high degree of noise that might make the signal incomprehensible to most listeners but not necessarily to sophisticated mathematical analysis.

---

In this chapter I have covered the importance of media in communication. There are three meanings of this term, with the boundaries between them not always clear. They are: organizations, recordings, and carriers or transmitters. All are important. When we undertake to send a message, whether to a single person or a multitude, whether once today or repeatedly over several centuries, we must consider a number of factors. These include the symbols that will be used to represent the message; the medium upon which those symbols will be recorded, if they are to be recorded; the means for transmitting from the place or time of origin to the destination; and what organization may be needed to produce or distribute the message.

Choosing the right media is as critically important to communication as the right seed is to farming or the right play selection in football. The originator must consider what he or she is going to work with and what is the best way to achieve the desired result. No wonder so few people are considered great communicators.

# Notes

1. Sellen and Harper, *The Myth of the Paperless Office.*

# Further Reading

## Media

Campbell, Martin, and Fabos. *Media & Culture.*
Fang. *A History of Mass Communication.*
Jamieson and Campbell. *The Interplay of Influence.*
Lavine and Wackman. *Managing Media Organizations.*
McLuhan. *Understanding Media.*
Winston. *Media Technology and Society.*

## Transmission Systems

Chandler. "The Transmission Model" (Web site).
Coogan and Smith. "Signal Transmission."
Lax. *Beyond the Horizon.*
Solymar. *Getting the Message.*

# 10

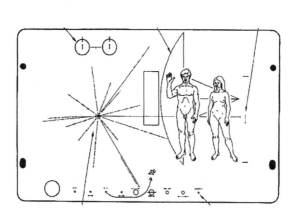

# Communicating Meaning
# and Understanding

What do we really mean by *meaning* or *understanding*? Like many
commonly used words, these can be hard to pin down to an exact
definition. Even asking what we mean by meaning is committing
the logical error of using the word *mean* to ask about *meaning,*
which suggests that we must know what *mean* means, even when
asking the question. Is that confusing enough? But it's very
important in communication to realize that what I *mean* by any
word or message can be quite different from what you *understand*
by it.

# Meaning

In a series of dictionary searches of the English language, I found a tendency to define *meaning* in terms of *intent*. A good example is "what is *intended* to be, or in fact is, signified, intended, referred to, or understood."[1] The italics were added. This leans toward, but does not actually say, that the meaning of a message is in the mind of the message originator. It is what that person intended that the recipient should understand by a message. I previously gave the example of my being bitten by a dog whose message seemed to me to be "Rub my belly," but which clearly did not mean that to him, since his attack was immediate and harsh when I tried to do as I thought I was asked.

A far more serious result of misunderstanding happened in New York City in 1999. There had been a shooting in one neighborhood and the police who investigated saw a man they felt they had reason to question. Reports differ, but one says the police approached the man and identified themselves, and the man reached for something in a pocket. The police took the gesture as reaching for a weapon and opened fire on him, releasing a fusillade of forty-one shots. Almost needless to say, the man died on the spot. Further investigation showed that all he had on him was a wallet, a pager, and a set of keys. In other words, he had no weapon, so his gestures could not have meant that he was reaching for one.

The legal resolution of this incident belongs to a jury. But one thing is very clear: whatever message the victim intended to send, it clearly was *not*, "I have a weapon." The message at least one police officer seems to have received was "I have a weapon and I might use it—on you." An apparently innocent man was killed. The reputation of a police force was tarnished.

In a situation like this, there isn't much time for either side to think. The man was a recent immigrant not used to the ways of police in his new country and apparently not aware of a recent shooting in his neighborhood. He did not have this information or the time to think what was the best way to respond to the police approach. The police, knowing there had been a shooting nearby and seeing what they took to be a hostile gesture, did not wait. They acted, tragically. Neither side knew the meaning of the message sent by the other. Neither had the time or knowledge to think things through.

## Understanding

What do we call meaning from the point of view of the person receiving a message? Again, a search of some dictionaries suggests an answer, although again not sharply defined. The word *under-standing* is often defined in terms of what the recipient of a message does, for example, "To perceive and comprehend the nature and significance of. . . ."[2] or "to grasp the meaning of."[3]

These approaches to *meaning* and *understanding* fit well in the Shannon model of communication described in chapters 5 and 9, differentiating between actions or thoughts by a message originator and its recipient. They bring out the critical importance of an originator thinking ahead. "How will my recipient perceive or comprehend this message?" By the way, I continue to italicize *meaning* and *understanding* to stress that the words used and how the words are perceived are under discussion, rather than the acts of intending or perceiving a meaning.

## Coming to Understanding

How do we, as recipients, decide what a message means, that is, what we will understand by it? How do we decide whether or not to believe it? There is generally considered to be two kinds of meaning: *lexical* and *grammatical*.

Lexical meaning, in a very formal sense, is the meaning in a vocabulary, the set of words used in a language. A lexicon is a dictionary, and dictionaries define meanings. The lexical meaning has also been formally defined as "the meaning of the base in a paradigm as *play* in *plays, played, playing*."[4] Since the very meaning of this definition is obscure to many readers, it serves as an illustration that an entry in a dictionary does not necessarily define a word for all readers.

Colin Cherry wrote

> The suggestion that words are symbols for things, actions, qualities, relationships, et cetera, is naive, a gross simplification. Words are slippery customers. The full meaning of a word does not appear until it is placed in its context. . . .[5]

Samuel and Alan Hayakawa put it more tersely, ". . . no word ever has exactly the same meaning twice."[6]

A culture at large, say a country or a portion of it, such as a profession, discipline, the south (of any country), a large metropolis, or even a small neighborhood, can also define meanings without the formality of a dictionary. The word *cool* means one thing in the context of temperature, another in the context of media (noted in chapter 9), yet another in modern slang where it means more or less good. So, in response to any of three messages: "What is the temperature?" "What kind of medium is this?" "I just won the lottery!" the response may all be the single word "cool" and this, in context, would be without ambiguity.

Essentially, then, the lexical meaning of a word is what we learn from others and is the meaning of the word more or less out of context. Grammatical meaning is meaning implied by the use of a word *in* context. The word *play*, for example, has several meanings. It can refer to a drama, to a planned series of moves in football or bridge, or to an activity entered into just for fun. You can play football and plan a specific play while doing so. The meanings are not the same.

A favorite illustration of use of word position and use of prior knowledge of lexical meaning is these two sentences:

> *Time flies like an arrow.*
> *Fruit flies like a banana.*

They may appear to have the same grammatical construction: noun, verb, adverb, article, noun, but they are not alike. In the first sentence the verb is *flies*, the subject is *time*. In the second the verb is *like* and means like to eat. We can usually understand all this because, if we are native speakers of English, we will often have heard the expression "time flies" and know it to mean that time seems to go by quickly, as does an arrow. We have probably heard of fruit flies, knowing they are a variety of insect. We use word position to give us the understanding that the subject precedes the verb, so we cannot treat sentence one as meaning that arrows fly like time. We use our knowledge of the world, our knowledge base, to assume there is no such insect as a time fly.

For another example, assume we have asked a friend if there is interest in seeing the local baseball team play the current league-leading team, loaded with stars we may never get another chance to see. He had thought to see a production of *Hamlet* on that day. When he makes up his mind whether to see Shakespeare or the star ball players he may say either

*I'd like to see the play.*

or

*I'd like to see them play.*

The meaning is made clear by the words *the* and *them*, in effect, by the presence or absence of the letter *m*. This also serves as an example of the importance of avoiding noise in a system.

A saying attributed both to Joseph Kennedy, father of President Kennedy, and to President Nixon was, "When the going gets tough, the tough get going." Here is another case, this time of two words, *tough* and *going*, each used twice, each time with a different meaning easily resolved by grammatical analysis. The first instance of *going* means *proceeding* or *carrying on*. The second instance of it means *started*, as in *getting started*. The first instance of *tough* means *difficult* and is an adjective. The second instance is a noun meaning tough or rugged people. The attractiveness of the sentence lies in its repeated use of words this way. Intentional use of words with multiple meanings is called a play on words. It is usually considered humorous, at least to those who know the various meanings and the context in which the word is being used—in other words, a select group. To them the humor may be calling attention to a serious point being made.

One of the great powers of natural language is that we can use it to change the meaning of a word as the sentence containing it proceeds. For example, "When I use the word *meaning* it refers to my intent when I composed the message containing it." That sentence is consistent with the view I have taken in this chapter, but it may not be accepted by everyone. However, any reader can see the new definition and understand that what follows is written with that understanding, whether or not the reader accepts the particular point of view. Small children, in my recollection around the age of six, like to play a game in which one says, "Yes means no and no means yes." It's fun up to a point, but I think I have never seen a child able to keep it straight for more than a minute or two without reverting to traditional usage. (Remember the discussion of the value of ambiguity in chapter 8.)

Having made all this about meaning and understanding perfectly clear, I now have to say it's not true all the time. (Exaggeration not intended to be taken literally is another example of multiple use of words. Here, *perfectly* really means "We both know that it's *not* perfectly clear." At least, I expect you to know that. But usually, at least in professionally written material, the basis on which communication takes place is the assumption that what is written or spoken *is* understood. Some artists, for example, insist that it is up to the viewers to decide what a painting means to them. The famous French painter Henri Matisse was quoted as saying he did not consider a picture complete until the viewer saw it and brought an interpretation to it.[7] Obviously, different viewers would surely interpret a painting differently. Other artists have expressed similar thoughts. They transfer to the viewer, the recipient, the right to decide what their message means. But everyone cannot do this. Imagine a football quarterback calling out some random numbers instead of a known play number and asking his teammates each to interpret them their own way. Imagine a doctor giving a patient a blank prescription form and telling him to decide what medicine to take. The Canadian artist Arthur F. Vickers put it in a way more consistent with how modern communications workers see it. He said, "In my tradition the artistic cycle is not complete until the art has been seen by others, until it has affected others."[8] In other words, the message not only has to be sent, but received and have had some effect. Marshall McLuhan, following his "medium is the message," said that the audience is the content, which fits right in with these artists's beliefs. It is the people receiving the message who decides what it means—for them.

There is a great controversy today about the meaning of the word *marriage*. We do not intend to enter into the religious issue of whether marriage should be sanctioned between two persons of the same sex, but to point out that leaving the determination of meaning to the recipient of a message, as do some painters, can result in bitter controversy, as we are seeing. To some, marriage is the union of a man and a woman and, indeed, is so defined in some dictionaries and laws. To others, the fact that the law may have said "between a man and a woman" is to be interpreted in modern times as "between two persons." After all, they might say, even though the Declaration of Independence states "all men are created equal," we now take this to mean both men and women and we take *equal* to mean equal in the eyes of the law, not equal in weight or lifting capacity, for example. The proposal that same-sex unions be granted all legal rights of marriage but should be called a "civil union" does not seem to work because one faction feels that denying the very use of the word *marriage* denies them equal rights. No lexicon or law, be it dictionary or Bible, will resolve this. Anyone can appeal to his or her own lexicon. Resolution will have to come by people coming together and agreeing what the meaning should be for people today.

We can once again redraw the Shannon model at this point (see figure 10.1 on next page). We now add a few more elements to show that a message originates in the knowledge base of the source and that the content of the message depends on what is in the knowledge base of the originator. The sender's knowledge base should be aware of what meaning it desires to send, what words or

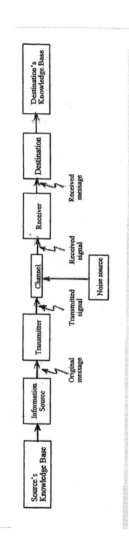

Figure 10.1. *Shannon model showing use of knowledge bases.* Both the originator and destination must draw on their respective knowledge bases to compose and interpret a meaningful message.

other symbols to use, what medium to use, and what will best be understood by the recipient. At the receiving end the destination's knowledge base must be used to understand what the received signals mean, which may involve knowing who sent it and under what circumstances. The two knowledge bases, of the sender and receiver, are critical parts of a communication. Note that in order to do what M. Matisse wanted—for the viewer to decide on meaning—that person's knowledge base had to include the information that some artists expect the viewer to make this decision and, therefore, not to try to figure out what the artist may have meant.

How do we go about deciding what a message means? How do we decide whether or not to believe it? Again, I have to say there is no simple answer. But it is a routine activity of many people to evaluate the message they receive, not just file it away or act upon it. Police detectives, bank loan officers, baseball players, doctors, storekeepers, and teachers and their students all must do it regularly.

The first step has to be to understand the basic symbols used in the received message—their lexical meaning. If there are words used or pictorial symbols that are not clear in their meaning we have a potential problem. Then the recipient must interpret the context, the grammatical meanings, of the message. A statement that food fish are available is different from one offering fish food.

Is there more than one possible interpretation? Earlier I used the example of a message calling for a meeting at 8 o'clock, that did not state whether it should be morning or evening. At the very least, the recipient should itemize the possibilities. In this case, there are only two—morning or evening. But, if place or date of the proposed meeting is unclear, there may be many possibilities.

Then decide which, if any, of the possible meanings make sense in terms of the recipient's knowledge of the sender and of the situation the message is about. Decades ago during the height of the Cold War there was a story often repeated about the detection of intercontinental missiles incoming to the United States. The story, as I heard it, was that a sergeant saw the indication on radar but could not believe it was the start of war because the world situation at the moment showed no sign of such drastic action. In fact, so the legend (or true story) goes, the radar images were reflections from the moon. The person who did *not* panic was right. The radar said war, but the sergeant's knowledge of the world said no war.

If the message is difficult to understand, could it have been made that way on purpose to foil attempts by unintended recipients to read it. This happens not just in spy stories or love notes passed in school. The recipient must consider whether the sender has a history of sending ambiguous messages. Or perhaps the sender is not adept at the language in which the message is composed. There is a Scottish legend about fighting between two clans. One had seized the castle of another while the castle forces' leader was away seeking help. Among the captives was the bagpiper of the castle, who was permitted to play on the ramparts of the castle because pipers were held in high regard, even by the enemy. In the distance the piper could see a boat carrying the absent leader returning home not knowing his home had been captured. The piper played an unfamiliar tune, heard by those in the boat. They wondered why they were being welcomed this way and decided that the unfamiliar tune was a signal.[9] What could it be signaling? "Keep away." So an unexpected, unfamiliar message was made clear.

Does all this sound like too much effort to put into reading and interpreting every message? It should not. In most cases we can go through these steps in an instant because there is no ambiguity. At other times, almost any effort is worth it—breaking an enemy code in war time, for example. Another real example came to me from a colleague at a university who was invited to give some lectures to a management class on searching the World Wide Web. She was warmly thanked for her efforts, but the inviting lecturer said the class did not really understand what was meant by evaluating a source. How can future business leaders not evaluate the source of messages reaching them, or even understand what the term means? Will they accept as true any statement about future markets, the quality of supplies to be purchased, or the background of a potential employee? Does it not matter who said so or what other messages may have to say?

## Understanding and the Knowledge Base

A knowledge base in our sense, remember, is the combination of everything a person has learned or has been genetically programmed to know or to know how to do. If we receive the message, "The world is flat," we know this is wrong or perhaps is a joke. If we heard our parents speaking, we as babies quickly learned to speak the same way—we learned their words, their meanings, and the grammar they used. If we get a message from a source our knowledge base tells us is reliable and it says that the distance from earth to the sun is 93 million miles, we file that away for future use, incorporate it in the base.

Perversely, although I stressed that the sender of a message wants the receiver to interpret it in a certain way, there are some complications to this. Some artists, as I pointed out, say, "This message means whatever it means to you. You decide."

## Brain Disorders

In some cases, how a message is interpreted may be a matter of genetics, injury, or illness. Any of these causes may affect how a message is interpreted, perhaps quite unexpectedly to the sender. One example is colorblindness. One form of this genetic condition makes people who have it unable to tell red from green. What does a red traffic light mean to them? Or green? They usually have to learn to interpret a signal based on which in the column of three lights is the one that is lit. Red is on top, so stop. Green is on the bottom, so it's okay to go. The color conveys no information to them. The position of the signals within the cluster of lights *must* be part of a colorblind person's knowledge base. Designers of

traffic signals should know this and stick to the standard arrangement of colors.

Another genetic condition that affects interpretation of
messages is called Williams syndrome. Among the symptoms of
this condition is that Williams people may not perceive and
remember a graphic image the way most of us do. Figure 10.2
shows an example. The letter D is formed from a set of Ys (a).
Normal people can view this image easily and reproduce both the
Ys and the D later from memory. Williams people tend to reproduce only the Ys but not the D as in b. In other words, they remember the detail but not the overall picture, the trees but not the forest.
People with a different genetic disorder, Down's syndrome, may
remember only the D, but not the Ys, as in c. There other genetic
aspects to how any of us interpret messages. As pointed out in
chapter 7, Chomsky's theory of a universal grammar is one, giving
all humans a basic framework for language. The dog's play bow
(chapter 8) is another example, giving all dogs a specific, universal
signal. Are there others? It is often hard to tell whether a particular
mental capability is something we learned or inherited but, either
way, it's part of the knowledge base.

**Task:**
REPRODUCE
IMAGE                 **Williams subjects**              **Down's subjects**

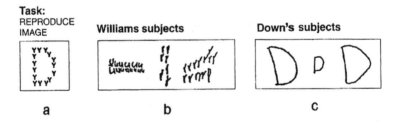

a                          b                          c

Figure 10.2. *Graphic used to test Williams and Down's syndrome sufferers.* The first image (a) presents the task—reproduce
this image from memory. The second image (b) shows typical
Williams subject results, a series of roughly drawn Ys but not the
D shape. The third image (c) shows results from typical Down's
subjects, clearly producing the D but not the Ys. Reproduced
courtesy of Dr. Ursula Bellugi.[10]

Another disease, amyotrophic lateral sclerosis (ALS), or Lou Gehrig's disease, gradually closes down the body's muscle system, but not the sensory organs. In its final stages, the disease may leave a person able to hear and feel but unable to communicate in any form. This is called being "locked in." There is some hope through experiments with brain waves controlled by what the person is thinking, not by muscles. A sufferer might be able to send signals through these waves, which could, at the very least, indicate a yes or no response to a question, hence send something like Morse Code messages by thinking of dots and dashes, or something. Think how it might feel to be able to hear what people say to you, feel their touch on your hand, but be completely unable to respond to them.

## Communicating across Cultures

One thing that should be clear by now is that to communicate from one person, animal, or machine to another there must be some shared knowledge. Those communicating must know the same meanings for symbols or at least know how to tell one another how to interpret a new symbol. I have shown examples of a message in grammatically incorrect English ("I ain't got no books.") that is perfectly clear, at least to native speakers who have heard this before. I have shown that drums that can only make two distinct sounds can be used to send words, not Morse code for words, when there is sufficient mutual understanding about what is probably being said. I have shown that languages without vowels, making many words ambiguous, can also be understood where there is common understanding of context.

What happens when two entities (humans or otherwise) try to communicate without some common base of understanding? Frank Ogden wrote about a computer language translator developed by the Fujitsu company in Japan. It could translate any of several spoken languages to any other. A test was conducted in which a person from Kenya speaking Swahili spoke with an Inuit in Canada speaking Inuktitut, through this translator.[11] What they said was not recorded, but consider the difficulties. The two might not have known anything about each other's country. But, at least we know they were human and we can assume they understood that a greeting would be appropriate and asking about each other's health and describing their respective families, all might be of interest. How much beyond this could they go? And how good was that translator, especially on understanding idioms?

For some time there has been fascination in the world with the possibility of communicating with beings in a different solar system in our galaxy and possibly a different galaxy. This is called communication with or the search for extra-terrestrial intelligence, CETI or SETI. We have no way to know if such beings exist and, if so, what they are like. Are they like us? Like dinosaurs? Like insects? Like nothing we can even imagine? Marvin Minsky, a noted artificial intelligence researcher, discussing this subject, pointed out, "If alien minds were entirely different from ours, communication might be impossible."[12] He then goes on to point out that if there are intelligent minds elsewhere, they are not likely to be *entirely* different from ours. The point is to find areas of common understanding. The philosopher Ludwig Wittgenstein put it that, "If a lion could talk we could not understand him."[13]

NASA once sent a spaceship bearing a message far out into our galaxy, hoping to open communications with extraterrestrial beings. What should the message say? Surely not a letter written in English!

As Minsky pointed out, there have to be some assumptions about the beings with whom we hope to communicate. If their level of intelligence, in our sense, is too low, we probably can't do it. NASA scientists led by Carl Sagan devised a plaque to put into the spaceship in the hope of opening communication with whoever found the ship. The content of the plaque is shown in figure 10.3 on the next page. The key features are a map of our solar system

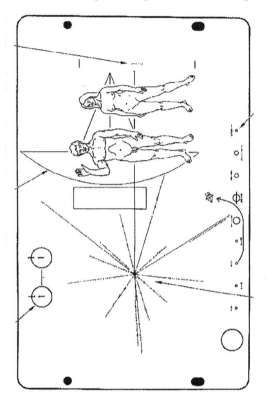

Figure 10.3. *The message sent into space by NASA.* A plaque containing these images was sent in NASA's *Explorer 10* spaceship in the hope of communicating with extraterrestrial beings elsewhere in our galaxy. A recipient has to make the assumptions that it is an attempt to communicate and that the originator is intelligent. Of course, the originator assumes the destination is also intelligent. It would help to know the physics of hydrogen atoms and that the man's gesture is means "peace." Some of the detail is not clear at this image size. Photo courtesy of the National Aeronautics and Space Administration (NASA).

at the bottom and the sun to the left, plainly shown appropriately scaled. Above the solar system, the radial image represents the directions from our sun to various pulsars (a form of star) of the galaxy. If the recipients are astronomers, this should be meaningful to them. Above the radial image is a diagram (two connected circles) representing a physical characteristic of hydrogen atoms. To the right of the radial is a sketch of the spaceship that carried the plaque and behind it figures that are, of course, a human man and woman. Their height is shown relative to the ship. The man is making a gesture that to many on earth means peace or good will. There is more detail than shows up well at this image size.

Now, the question is will our space neighbors understand all this? Will they understand enough to recognize an attempt to communicate, even if all symbols are not clear? Would they recognize the man's gesture as one of peace or could they see it as one they use when about to attack? It is reasonable to assume that intelligent beings exist throughout the universe. But would they know astronomy? Might they be vastly different in size, shape, and sensory organs or technology? Maybe this was not the best message to send. But what would have been better? Once again, we must remember the importance of symbols recognized by sender and receiver and think what effect our message is likely to have on anyone reading it, *and* we must be humble enough to recognize that we cannot answer all the questions.

---

What I have tried to bring out here is that merely sending a message, even if it's received, is not enough. The sender normally has to think what he or she intends to say and how the recipient is likely to understand it. The recipient has to think what it appears to mean, calling on his or her knowledge of the sender, the conditions under which it is sent, and knowledge of the world. Merely successful transmission is not enough.

# Notes

1. *Webster's New World Dictionary of the American Language.*
2. *American Heritage Dictionary.*
3. *Webster's Third International Unabridged Dictionary.*
4. *Merriam-Webster Online Dictionary.*
5. Cherry, *On Human Communication.*
6. Hayakawa and Hayakawa, *Language in Thought and Action*, p. 39.
7. Schneider. (Television interview with Charlie Rose.)
8  Vickers, "Opening Address."
9. Mackay, *A Collection,* pp. 11–12.
10. Lenhoff et al., "Williams Syndrome and the Brain."
11. Ogden, *The Last Book*, p. 41
12. Minsky, "Communication with Alien Intelligence."
13. Wittgenstein, *Philosophical Investigations*, p. 223.

# Further Reading

## Meaning and Understanding

"Amadou Diallo Case" (Web site about NYC shooting).
"Detective Bullets Fell from Diallo's Body" (Web site).
Devlin. *Infosense.*
Hayakawa and Hayakawa. *Language in Thought and Action.*
Jian. "Organizational Knowledge and Learning' (Web site).
"Nebraska K-12 Reading/Writing Framework" (see Strand 4 at this
      Web site—Meaning and Understanding.)
Richards and Ogden. *The Meaning of Meaning.*
"World: America's Police Shoot at Unarmed Man 41 Times" (Web
      site).

## Brain Disorders

Adler. *Lou Gehrig.*
"Disorders of Muscle Stimulation."
Lenhoff et al. "Williams Syndrome and the Brain."
Lerner. "Communicating via Brain Waves."

Parker. "Reading Minds."
Rosner. *Understanding Williams Syndrome.*
"Williams Syndrome Association" (Web site).

## Extraterrestrial Communication

Billingham and Pesek. *Communication with Extraterrestrial Intelligence.*
Sagan. *Carl Sagan's Cosmic Connection.*
Shostak and Barnett. *Cosmic Company: The Search for Life.*
Swift. *SETI Pioneers.*

# 11

# Communication: The Full Monty

"Full monty" is a British expression meaning "the whole thing." We have looked at communication from several points of view so far. Now, let's look at the whole thing, the entire process of composing and sending meaningful messages and achieving the results we want to achieve.

Warren Weaver, a colleague of Claude Shannon, wrote about three levels of communication.[1] The first he called the *technical level,* which is mostly concerned with the mechanics of transforming a message into a signal, transmission of the signal, and re-transforming it at the receiver. The second is the *semantic level,* which is concerned with meaning and with whether the recipient understands the way the sender wanted to be understood. The third is the *effectiveness level,* which is concerned with what happens when the recipient gets the message. Did the person come to the meeting at the correct time? Did a ship come to the rescue of the sinking *Titanic*? Did the person simply enjoy listening to some music or a comedy? Or did the sender want the recipient to do some particular thing but nothing happened? The comments of artists mentioned in chapter 10 fit this model of communication quite well.

We might even want to add another aspect of the originator's work: composition, which is the formation of the message and is done before we get to the technical level of transmission. Now we can redraw Shannon's model one last time (figure 11.1). This time, I show both the information source and the destination as cloud-like, rather than distinct, well-defined entities. This is to stress that sending a message is not the simple act of saying, "Okay, I have a message. Here it is." It may involve many people or one person in many steps. If many, then more than one knowledge base is involved—more than one way of perceiving any situation. Similarly, receipt is not merely opening the e-mail letter. It involves interpretation, evaluation, assimilation, *and* possibly taking some action, even if just to acknowledge receipt, perhaps only to consciously refuse to do what was asked.

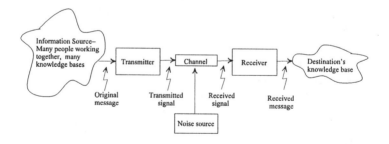

Figure 11.1 *Shannon model, with multiple originators.* Other than personal letters, messages often require more than one person to be involved in composition, hence more than one knowledge base (KB). Similarly, at the destination end more than one person may be involved in interpretation, even if only interpreting an entry in a reference book.

The effect of receipt of a message may not be solely on the person who receives it. In commercial media there can also be an effect on advertisers interested in how many people receive their message and what their characteristics are—rich, poor, conservative, liberal, old, young, etc. Advertisers are then interested in such measures of effect as who or how many saw the material sent, how well it held their attention, and what they did afterward with regard to the product, services, or candidates offered.

# Composition

Major politicians do not usually write their own speeches. They have to communicate with the people they hope will vote for them, but they are often too busy and they can hire people who are very good at getting across the meaning the politician wants to get across. Being a good decision maker and a respected leader does not necessarily mean being an effective communicator.

An auto maker, say the Ford Motor Company, does not ask its engineers who design cars to write scripts for television advertising and then film them. This work is done by professional advertising people.

Anyone who writes, whether it is a political speech, an advertisement, or a script for a television comedy program, must be skilled not only at getting ideas but at knowing how to express them to the intended audience and by way of the intended media. In politics, does the audience understand enough about taxes for the leader to explain in five minutes what the proposed new tax plan is and why it is a good one. A comedy writer for television who wants to include some local jokes about the place where the broadcast originates must be sure that people not from the local community can understand them. If making jokes about the size of mosquitoes in Alaska, will an audience in Georgia appreciate the joke?

What is the best medium to use? Presenting a "talking head" on television is not the best way to hold audience attention. But

should the president of a country use charts? Will people understand them? Would the audience consider it undignified for a
president to use charts in a talk? There is not much question that
the best way to communicate the action of a football game is by
television because the cameras give close-ups of action, multiple
viewing angles, and breadth of image. The more cameras the more
that can be seen. Further, important scenes can be re-run for the
audience. Some stadiums now provide these television images to
the live audience, but without the giant screens, the on-the-spot
audience may see less of the game than the viewer at home. One
sports writer[2] once said that radio was the best way to "see" a
baseball game. But that assumes the listener knows the game well,
probably knows the stadium in which it is being played, and knows
the players. Then he imagines what he cannot see. To a person who
does not know the game well, the radio version may be meaningless.

## Technical Considerations

The originator of a message must consider some of the technical
aspects of how the message will be converted to a signal, accuracy
of conversion and transmission, speed of transmission, and modes
of presentation after reception. The originator does not always get
involved in conversion, but might, for example, when trying to
send a representation of a painting through a black-and-white fax
machine. What will it look like at the other end? Should the artist
even allow transmission if the black and white, low-resolution
medium might lose key elements of the original? Should a motion
picture director or producer allow a black and white film to be
colorized? The color will not be highly realistic and the artistic
effects of lighting and contrast in the original may be lost.

Speed is usually easy. How long will it take to get the message
to its destination? In 18th-century America, mail was not routinely
delivered to the west, and the west began not too far from the
Atlantic Ocean. A sender of a letter might have had to be content

to give the letter to someone intending to go near the destination. How long would it take? There was no knowing. In the 19th century, there were stage coaches for mail going west (now *really* west, to the Pacific Coast) and there was the Pony Express, then the telegraph, and then the transcontinental railroad. The telegraph was by far the fastest, but if the lines were cut anywhere along the way, the sender would not know what happened and possibly never know whether the message got through.

Accuracy is extremely important. Suppose you are a newspaper correspondent in a foreign country. You want to send a message to the paper using an old-fashioned telegraph system where the operator will retype your text. Will it be received as originally written? It matters. I once sent a telegram in English from Casablanca, Morocco, to London, England, explaining, a delayed flight and closing with the sentence, "Don't wait up." It arrived as "Do wait up."

In modern times, we have print, telephone, radio, television, the Internet (e-mail and the World Wide Web), the regular mail service (sometimes, perhaps unfairly, called snail mail), and the express mail services such as FedEx and UPS. Choosing the best way to send a message becomes more and more difficult as new methods are invented and more and more of us want messages delivered as soon as possible without having to risk their loss. Yet, airplanes carrying mail crash, ships sink, and computers fail or are sabotaged by viruses. Risk of losing a message en route is always there to some extent.

# Semantics

Semantics has to do with meaning. But, as I've said before, the meaning of any message can be different for different people. If the originator wants it to have some particular effect on the destination, then he or she must think about how the recipient will think about it. If you're a writer, cheerleader, catcher in baseball, or a boy about to ask a girl for a date for the first time, the burden is on you to make sure you are going to be understood.

The recipient has to do three things: interpret, evaluate and assimilate, often simultaneously. The incoming message must be interpreted. What does it seem to be saying? Then, it must be evaluated. Should it be believed? Then it has to be assimilated, combined with the destination's existing knowledge. Now, you don't do all this consciously when listening to a stand-up comic. You laugh or not, but you don't tend to evaluate. But when you hear about a great deal for a used stereo or car, when someone tells you that steroids will help your athletic performance and no one will ever know you're taking them, or you should delete a certain file from your computer, you had better evaluate your source. These messages could be false. Assimilation, remember, means to integrate the new message into your knowledge base (to what you already know). Does it conflict? Does it add to your knowledge? Does it fail to connect with anything in your own experience? You have to make sense of the message, sometimes easily and immediately, sometimes only with difficulty and taking a long time.

# Effectiveness

In some situations where people taking part are limited to a relatively few highly trained persons, effectiveness can be extremely important. This can be a football team where the quarterback calls plays in a code that everyone is supposed to know. This tells each player what to do, reduces the time it might otherwise take to get this message across, and keeps it secret from the opposing team. In aviation, a pilot and an air traffic controller on the ground have conversations loaded with jargon—words with specialized meaning known only to aviation people, though not secret. This allows for precise meanings in short conversations since time may important, for example, to bring a plane in for a landing in bad weather or to avoid a collision. Long-winded conversations in either of these examples could be harmful. English is an almost universal language for air traffic control, but not all controllers or pilots are fluent in it.

The European Association of Aerospace Industries (EAAI) has produced a book of simplified English to be used mostly by aircraft maintenance people. Why is it needed? Because airplanes are made in only a few countries of the world, but are used in many countries. Not all maintenance technicians can understand idiomatic English. This book includes some grammatical rules and a great many rules for what word to use for a given meaning. For example, it is common in English to use the word *follow* to mean obey or conform to, as in "Follow the safety precautions." The EAAI text specifies that *follow* means only "to come after." To insist on adherence to a rule, use the word *obey*.[3]

What happens when things do not go right, when the quarterback throws the ball but no one from his team is there to receive it, or when a pilot suddenly sees another plane coming toward him? Analysis later can probably tell what went wrong. One player either didn't hear the signal or didn't understand its meaning; or an air controller's message to the pilot to change his altitude similarly was not heard or was not understood. Analysis later, even though it determines the cause, may come after a plane crash or loss of a football playoff game. In any cases like this we can ask the following questions:

• Did the sender say the right thing, and say it clearly? Did the sender know whether the recipient would understand the language, jargon, or codes used?
• Did the transmission system carry the signal without error? Did noise interfere? Did slurred words or an unusual accent by a speaker cause ambiguity?
• Did the players or pilot know all the codes and special words?
• Did the players or pilot do the correct thing when they heard the message? If not, why not?

## Some Real-Life Examples

Here are three examples of communication; the first two have
existed since writing was invented; the third is quite modern. The
first, writing an essay, is an activity of one person, as would be
painting a picture or composing a symphony. The second, a
conversation, involves at least two people, but each is the sole
creator of his or her own messages. The third, a television advertisement, involves many people. TV is known as a collaborative
medium. Yes, on rare occasion a single person can make a film, but
it's hardly the usual thing. The same goes for publishing a newspaper or broadcasting a radio program. These all need teams, some
quite large and the success of the project may depend as much on
how well the team works together as on the creative genius of any
one member.

### Writing an Essay

Suppose you are filling out an application for admission to a
university or applying for a job. One question asked is why you
want to attend this school or work for this company.

What are the communication issues here? You've been asked
a question. Do you understand what it means? For example, do you
think the meaning is that your reasons for wanting this position in
school or work are what will decide on your acceptability? Could
it be that the real meaning (i.e., originator's intent) is to see how
well you write? And, if that is the case, would you write a different
answer than you might have if you thought you were simply
supposed to list the good things about the school or company from
your point of view? If you only make that list, you may do yourself
out of being selected. On the other hand, perhaps you are being
asked how much you bothered to find out about the institution and
they would like to admit or hire only candidates who take the
trouble to really find out about them.

We cannot resolve this issue because every school or company
may have a different intent in asking the question. We can,

however, point out how important it is to understand the meaning of the question your are asked to answer.

When composing an original paper, opinion article, essay, or thesis, there is usually not a specific question to answer. The questions must be raised within the paper. It becomes even more important to make clear what issues or questions are being addressed. When reporting on research work in a thesis, it is also necessary to lay out the procedures used, the data collected, the analytical methods used, and the results of any analysis. The author should anticipate, to the extent possible, what the reader would want to know, and provide answers.

In short, a great deal of planning and some research is needed to write a convincing essay.

## Conversation

You are going to meet a friend at a coffee house. There is no agreed-upon agenda. You would expect to relax, drink some good coffee, and talk. In such a situation you would not normally prepare a speech. Nor would you have much time to ponder what to say when your friend has said something expecting to hear your reaction. Still, you have things to think about. Noise level—are you easily able to hear each other? Privacy—do you want to lower your voice so others cannot hear you? And if you do, can your friend still hear you? Even though you are good friends, are there subjects that it would be best to avoid? Politics? Why she recently broke up with her boyfriend? Is the boyfriend now fair game for you? There may be other topics it is best to avoid, yet candor between friends is expected as long as it is tempered with tact.

These are not questions that require much preparation. Your knowledge base knows or assumes it knows the answers. The very fact that the conversation is spontaneous, even if avoiding a few topics, is what makes it relaxing and enjoyable.

## Television: Content, Transmission, Effectiveness

Let us is assume we are watching the entire process of creating an advertisement to be shown on television at a later date, after which there will be some measurement of audience reaction.

*Preparation*

Before the performance (the performance contains the message sent to viewers) the following steps are taken or questions answered:

1. The advertisers decide on the target audience. If this is to be for a luxury car, that means viewers probably over 30 years of age and in an upper income bracket. It may be directed primarily toward men or primarily toward women.

2. They must decide when the ad is to be shown—time of day, day of the week, time of year. Prime time costs more and attracts different users than daytime television, so a choice must be made. How long will the ads take to run? What shows should it be connected with—news, football, games, serious drama, or situation comedies?

3. Where or in what context will the action or product be shown? Automobile manufacturers love to show their cars on scenic roads with no other traffic in spring or summer regardless of the date the ad is to be shown. Or it might be a winter scene showing the heroic car zooming through six inches of snow as if on a dry road. If the action is to be done in a studio, what scenery is needed?

4. Who will the actors be? Known figures? Professional stunt performers? Actors represented as average men or women on the street?

5. What is the basic message? That the product is new? Better than before? More attractive? Giving prestige to the owner? Safer?

Given the basic decisions, writers draft scripts, designers select a set or location, casting directors hire the performers, technical crews, and equipment to be assembled.

## Performance

This is the presentation of the message that will go to the audience. There will be rehearsals, "takes," and retakes. The message will be recorded; advertisements are rarely broadcast live.

Sound and video are separately recorded, most likely on the same magnetic tape. Some video and some audio segments from archival files may be combined later with the live action, and the "voice-over" can be dubbed in.

There are probably several cameras in use, requiring a director to decide what each should be focused on. There is a mini-communications network that enables the director to see what each camera is seeing and to talk to any camera operator.

Later, all the material, whether recorded from live performance, voice-overs, or archival footage, is combined by an editor into one smoothly (they hope) flowing presentation. All ends up on tape or possibly on a disk.

## Conversion and Transmission to Broadcasters

Audio is recorded as you, yourself, might do with a home tape recorder. Sound waves become electrical signals by the action of a microphone.

Color video images, as described in chapter 4, are split into three single-color images by use of color filters: red, blue, or green. The intensity of the light waves of each color is converted to electrical signals

The recording of colored images is done onto the tape, which must have separate tracks for audio and each of the three colors. This is what goes from the studio to individual broadcasting stations. At the station they will find accompanying material telling at what time to display the ads, what programs they should be attached to, the number of repetitions, etc. Another option is to distribute material by converting it to radio signals and transmitting these up to a satellite and then down to the station that will record it and ultimately broadcast it.

*Transmission to the Final Destination*

Eventually, the disk with the advertisement arrives at the television station that will broadcast it. It may then go "over the air" to the home from a local transmitter or via satellite.

At every stage, from original taping to final showing, there is some opportunity for noise to creep in. The combination of better receivers, cable transmission, and digital rather than analog signals reduces noise considerably over what we once had to deal with, but the possibility is always there. Live telecasts of news from war zones or sports events often show momentary loss of full images replaced by a repeated still image or large single-color pixels replacing many smaller ones, each of which had many colors, thus removing detail from an image as in figure 11.2. This is not caused by the content but by the large number of electrical connections that must be set up for remote televising, hence larger than normal possibility for error.

 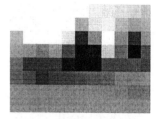

Figure 11.2. *Distortion of a TV image.* We see this happen occasionally when a portion of a signal is lost, typically when picking up news from a distant place and sometime sports events. Instead of thousands of pixels we see just a few, each of a single color. The portion of the message that was lost tells the receiver how to interpret the image data. It is usually impossible to tell what the image is, however, the effect normally lasts only a few seconds. Photos by the author.

*Receiver*

After all the various conversions of signals, we are almost done. A television signal coming from a satellite is like the one coming over the air from the local transmitter but at a higher frequency. Both are converted to electric current in the receiving antenna. If the signal comes from cable, it is already in electrical form and with higher gain (stronger signal) than from the antenna. Either way, the audio part of the electrical signal is converted to sound through electro-magnet controlled diaphragms in the speakers. The three video tracks (red, blue, green ) illuminate portions of pixels with intensity corresponding to what the camera saw at production time, as described in chapter 4.

*Destination*

We are now back to considering how the destination person reacts to the message. Advertising is created for effect, not for the sake of art. Hence, we become interested in:

• Did the viewer understand the message?
• Did the viewer stay with the program rather than change channels? Of particular interest to advertisers—did the viewer of the scheduled program stay to see the ads or take those opportunities to go for a beer, or change channels?
• Did the viewer like or appreciate the basic show? This leads to the question: will the viewer want to see more programs like this?
• Did the viewer buy the advertised product?

---

The point of this chapter has been to make clear that communication is never as simple a matter as putting a stamp on a letter, dialing a telephone, or typing an e-mail address. We always have to think about Weaver's technical, semantic, and effectiveness levels of communication: how to transmit and receive, the content or meaning of a message, and its effectiveness or what it accomplishes. We must also remember that many forms of communication require many people working together as a team.

# Notes

1. Weaver, "Some Recent Contributions."
2. Smith, *The Storytellers.*
3. *AECMA Simplified English.*

# Further Reading

## Communication Theory

Cherry. *On Human Communication.*
Devlin. *Infosense.*
Durham and Kellner. *Media and Culture Studies.*
Weaver. "Some Recent Contributions."

## Writing

Broderick. *The Able Writer.*
Neeld. *Writing.*

## Production and Distribution in Media

Campbell. *Technical Film and TV for Nontechnical People.*
Dominick. *The Dynamics of Mass Communication.*
Gerbarg. *The Economics, Technology, and Content.*
Goodwin and Whannel. *Understanding Television.*
Harriss. *The Complete Reporter.*
Newsom and Wollert. *Media Writing.*
"NTSC Tutorials, Free" (Web site on basic TV).
O'Donnell, Benoit, and Hausman. *Modern Radio Production.*
Straubhaar and LaRose. *Communications Media in the Information Society.*

# 12

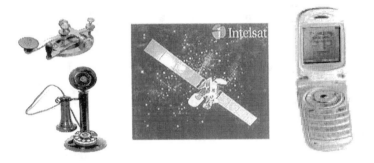

# Communication Systems of Today and Tomorrow

One of the outstanding features of the 20th century was the rate of change in our communication systems. Remember that before the 18th century the only ways we could record messages were by writing letters, scrolls, or books, carving messages in stone or wet clay, or printing them. These had to be carried to a destination or displayed publicly for all to see. We had, of course, sound and light for carrying speech, other noises, and visual signals, but only over limited distances. The only way to send a message, say from England or Spain to one of their colonies on the other side of the world, was by ship, which could take months and possibly never even arrive.

During the 18th century ships got bigger and faster. Navigational instruments improved so that communication across oceans became faster and more certain.

In the 19th century, we began to use steam to propel ships at sea and trains on land. These significantly reduced the time involved in sending messages over long distances and increased the safety or probability of the message arriving at all. In that same century we began use of electricity for messages, first in the telegraph and then in the telephone. These inventions further increased delivery speed of messages, increased the probability of their safe arrival, and increased the number of messages sent and received. The telephone in particular gave people a sense of nearness, even when quite apart physically, because first time users could talk directly to people who were beyond the range of the sound-carried human voice and they could recognize the voice talking back to them.

In the 20th century there were two or maybe three main developments. Two were technological: radio, or more generally the use of electronics to generate electromagnetic waves to transmit messages, and aviation, a far faster way to deliver the messages or messengers than trains, ships, or automobiles. Electronics also brought us television, communication satellites, cell phones, computers, and miniaturization of most communication equipment. The third development, which is somewhat controversial, is the creation of the *global village,* which is based on use of all communications technology but mostly on the two main ones of the 20th century—electromagnetic transmission of signals and computers.

Now in the early part of the 21st century, we are beginning an era of personalization of the electronic means of sending messages and freedom from reliance on wires to connect us with the various means of communication. Personalization came both from the introduction of wireless transmitters and receivers and lowering the cost of these devices and from an increased felt need to be constantly in touch with home, friends, or office. Was the need real, or did it result from advertising and intriguing gadgets?

# The Wired City

At some time in the late 20th century people began to talk and write about a "wired city." This meant that we were connected by wire to what seemed an incredible number of people, places, and services. We had the telephone, automatic teller machines (ATMs), and the Internet to connect us with banks, libraries, grocery stores, news agencies, entertainment, schools, museums, . . . and the list goes on almost endlessly. Use of wires meant we did not have to visit in person.

What has the wired city given us? Mostly interconnectedness. We are linked by wire to many people and institutions: our friends and relations, important emergency services, banks (even if we have to go a few blocks to the nearest ATM), the Internet, and radio and television broadcasts. Radio mostly comes over the air, not by wire, but it is an honorary part of the wired city. Television signals, originally also over the air, are now often sent through cable, a form of wire. Our wires reach the individuals we most want to talk with—emergency help, stores and banks, government offices, and news and entertainment. We are a communicating society and the wired city seems the ultimate degree of connectedness.

Having achieved a wired city, we are now on the verge of doing away with a need for all these wires. Cell phones, now called wireless or mobile phones, and satellite television, which can be used for Internet connection, are leading the way. But the wire forces will not give up easily. The coaxial cable used by television is highly reliable and has great bandwidth, allowing us not only to receive television images and sound but to connect our computers as well. Local telephone companies keep finding new ways to transmit high-bandwidth signals, enabling them to provide services, such as Internet connections and movies, over existing phone lines.

Wire is not only reliable but also secure. Yes, it is possible to tap a wire, but not nearly as easy as it is to intercept a signal using a radio receiver alone. And, wire is not as subject as radio is to problems with the weather such as thunderstorms that generate electromagnetic waves that are more likely to affect those systems that send signals over the air. Both infrared and radio frequency signals going over the air may be affected by rain or cloud cover. A new form of wire is the fiber optic cable, which we described in chapter 4 and is immune to most environmental interference. The world is becoming increasingly interconnected with these glass fibers, not only from city to city but from country to country and continent to continent, under the oceans. Once installed, they are extremely reliable, provide enormous bandwidth, and are inexpensive to use. Unfortunately, their near-universal installation can be expensive.

In spite of the enormous number of cables installed from city to city, country to country, and even office building to office building within the city, what we do not yet have is optical fiber coming into our individual homes to connect wired telephones and perhaps even computers and televisions. We will probably be seeing this soon, and when we do the cost of communication should go down significantly. That means we will probably see an increase in use of all sorts of communication equipment.

## The Wireless World

What started as radio-telephones became cell phones, whose sellers began to call them the more prestigious-sounding wireless or mobile phones. These may well do away with the wired city. In its place will be the wireless world, no longer bound by our ability to string copper or even glass wire between us and those with whom we want to communicate. Although wired telephones are still widely used in the developed world in places where there previously had been minimal or no telephone service, it is both easier and cheaper to install mobile telephone service rather than wires. While telephone companies used to take responsibility for repair of their phones wherever installed, now they tend to stop their service at the wall of the house. Any service inside is paid for by the consumer. In short, maintaining wire service is a pain in the neck and the phone companies are glad to be rid of it.

Mobile telephones have added features (see chapter 4). They can become transmitters and receivers for text messages and graphic images, as well as cameras and computers. This seems on the way to becoming the dominant mode of communication. Some come with a built-in radio or musical disk player. They could be made to receive television signals, but without the 50-inch screens becoming popular today. Perhaps it could become a projection TV, allowing any convenient wall to be the display device.

For most of us in the wired city the wireless world is nearly here, if we want it. It gives us unprecedented freedom to communicate without having to be at a fixed location. In Paris an experiment was begun in 2003 to install antennas in public places for wireless connections between portable computers or mobile telephones and the Internet. These are now found in many airports, hotels, and even coffee shops  in other countries as well. This system is something like the cell phone system, but the connections from the user's computer are made directly to the Internet service provider, not to the telephone system that would then have to connect the user to the Internet. The service can also be provided on trains and, of course, railroad stations and hotels. This makes access to the Internet more like a public utility available to everyone. That is, you would pay for what you use but not for the right to access it.

Unfortunately, there is often a downside to new technology. When hurricane Katrina struck New Orleans in 2005, we were reminded that cell phones are radios that talk to a receiver fairly close to the phone user. These receivers are then connected to the conventional telephone system. Wires and electric current are involved. When telephone wires and electric power were cut by the storm, cell phones no longer worked in many areas and emergency services were often left without communication.

# Personal Communication

While once we usually found only one of any kind of electrical communication device in each home or office, this gradually has changed. With extension telephones there could be several in one house and each person in an office could have one. As radios became inexpensive and small, they began to be found in almost every room of many houses. Televisions, too, have proliferated and are now often found in the living room, the family room, several bedrooms within a house, and, lately, in the family van as well. Many households now have a cell phone for each family member.

When computers originally came into the home, they were not treated as communication devices by the average user. But at about the same time that cell phones became popular, so did e-mail, then the full Internet and the World Wide Web. What these changes did was to give an individual user the ability to communicate with people or organizations worldwide at the user's convenience. Time zones did not matter. Messages could be recorded at the receiving end and respondents could read or hear and respond to them when they had time. The exchange of messages between countries half a world apart could easily be done in one day or less. Every user of a computer could now visit the sites of his or her choice (well, within rules set by parents, libraries, schools, or employers). Even in television use, first the VCR and later the digital set-top box gave each user the opportunity to record a program and to play it back at his or her convenience.

If we owned the maximum kind of wireless, mobile telephone, we could talk, send and receive text messages, send and receive pictures, play games, or compute whenever we wanted.

But it may be hard for today's users of wireless telephones and television set-top boxes to think what it must have been like when the telephone and radio were one to a family and when radio and, later, television entertainment came at standard times only and the entire family had to agree on (or argue about) what to watch. We will probably never revert to those days.

Is there a drawback to this degree of personalization? In some ways, yes. We lose the common experience of everyone who works or goes to school together or just hangs out together to have seen a program in their own homes at the same time and be able to talk about it the next morning. That means less shared experience with friends, less conversation, and less practice in speaking in groups. Reliance on the ease of use of cell phones may reduce the amount of personal contact we have with friends, relations, and people with whom we do business. In McLuhan's terms, conversation is a cool medium. Each participant must take an active part, think, and express his or her thoughts. Receiving entertainment through television or movies is hot; the user relaxes and lets the medium do the work.

## The Global Village

It was Marshall McLuhan, again, who first proposed that we have a global village. This meant we could talk with almost anyone anywhere. But more than just that, we could exchange voice conversations, pictures, movies, music, and art. We could form groups of compatible people, all over the world. Cultural ideas did not remain in one country, they could spread around the world. For example, you see in the news pictures that young men over much of the world dress similarly in T-shirts and jeans, often the shirts carrying names of American athletic teams. In some countries, young women are far more constrained by tradition and even law in the clothing they wear. Rock and roll music has spread the world over, not always to the liking of an older generation. English has spread as an almost universal language. We are no longer limited to our immediate neighbors for friendship, source of ideas, or styles.

A global village can consist of self-selected members. They may be related by interest in music or soccer, age or profession, or whatever. Members may completely ignore other members they do not agree with or like personally.

A village in the traditional sense consists of a group of people who live near each other and at some distance from other villages, towns, or cities. There was no exact meaning to *near* or *some distance*, but *near* had to mean close enough for frequent contact with other members of the village and *some distance* had to mean far enough that village members did not meet members of other villages often. In such a village, most members would share many characteristics. Most may have in common race, religion, national origin, or perhaps politics. There will be tolerance for a certain amount of variation. If there were a town drunkard, he or she would be tolerated and the family helped. If there were one Republican in a Democratic town (or vice versa), that person would be tolerated. Not everyone would like everyone else, but every-one would know they all lived in the same village and had to get along, the rich and poor, the religious and irreligious, the sober and the drunk. A member of such a village typically could not walk downtown without greeting every co-member encountered on the walk.

This picture of a village in the geographic sense is not like the global village. Such a village cannot consist just of doctors or lovers of rap music, for example. There is no requirement to "get along" with people who are different or merely disliked. Yes, there are global villages, but they are not like the geographic villages or neighborhoods in which we live.

## Convergence

Convergence means coming together as a lens focuses light rays to converge at a point or shoppers converge on a sale table at department store. In communication it has two rather different meanings, which are not always made clear when the word is used. In general, it means communications media coming together. How? There are two general ways.

First, there is physical or technical convergence which, in this sense, means transmitters or receivers able to handle more than one kind of signal. For example, some computer printers can serve as either a copier or a fax unit, and a wireless telephone can handle pictures, text, and sound. All these are different media converging into a single transmitter or receiver that can tell what kind of signal is to be sent or is being received and perform the appropriate conversions to bring the message to the recipient.

An important example of technical convergence is the hand-held, palmtop, Blackberry, or similar gadgets with different names. It typically allows its use as a computer. It can handle e-mail and the new text messages or Short Message Service. It can include a camera and can transmit images. It can be attached to a projector displaying computer-stored images, allowing it to be used for people giving lectures or presentations. How does all this differ from the advanced form of cell phone? Not much.

In the 1990s systems were introduced that allowed voice telephone conversations to be conducted over the Internet. They cost little more than use of the Internet itself. But they didn't work too well and gradually fell out of use. Now new systems are being developed that allow voice conversations via the Internet at no or little charge. Major North American telephone companies have begun offering or experimenting with offering this kind of service. Telephones would have to be connected to the telephone line or cable that handles Internet connections, but calls could be made to any telephone anywhere. This is another example of convergence in the technical sense. For the telephone companies, this could mean far less expense in maintaining lines and switching centers, which could be translated into lower subscriber costs.

A second meaning of convergence and has to do with organiza-tion. Organizational convergence occurs when two or more media organizations combine to offer two or more services. For example, a television network buys an athletic team in order to provide the content—the game and its advertising revenue—as well as the distribution services and their revenue. Telephone companies buy television cable distributors. Time Inc., a magazine producer, first combined with Warner Brothers, a motion picture maker and distributor, to offer a combined broader range of services. Then Time Warner combined with CNN (a cable news content provider and distributor). Later, America Online (AOL) combined with the expanded Time Warner to merge all the various Time Warner and CNN services with AOL's Internet services, all supposedly helping each other. Unfortunately, this worked out to be, according to the *New York Times*, "one of the worst mergers in American business history." Shares in the combined company tumbled and the name of the company was changed from AOL Time Warner to Time Warner.[1] Convergence of this type is not automatically a good thing for business or consumers. The combined companies get to be too big and their managers may not have the specialized experience that each medium needs. In some cases the converging unit has fallen apart or sold off its newly acquired components. They may also become so powerful as to be able to control markets or convince courts that they can. Examples of large companies that have been brought to court on antitrust charges were the American Telephone and Telegraph Co. (AT&T) and Micro-soft.

But technical convergence seems to work in most cases, giving individual users more options than previously available, such as use of less equipment or more kinds of services. Notable successes have been the previously mentioned multifunction computer printers, mobile telephones, and the Internet, which can now deliver radio broadcasts and movies as well as the more conventional computer-stored files.

# Adaptation

When anything new enters our lives, we must usually change our behavior to accommodate it or adapt to it. In chapter 1 I cited a quot-ation from Plato decrying the introduction of writing to society because it limited memory and gave to its users the appearance of wisdom, not the reality of it. Literature and teaching, at the time, were mainly oral; writing seemed merely a mechanical substitute for the ability to speak and remember. Later, when mechanical printing was first introduced in Europe, Jacob Burckhardt reported that ". . . the sudden appearance of printed books was greeted at first with anything but favor. The envoys of Cardinal Bessarion, when they saw for the first time a printed book in the house of Constatine Lascaris, laughed at the discovery 'made among the barbarians in some German city,' and Federigo of Urbino [a noted collector of *handwritten books* at the time] would have been ashamed to own a printed book."[2]

Much later, the telephone seemed to become an instant hit wherever installed, but it still required some getting used to. In 1882 it was the Germans' turn to scorn. A proposed lecture to business executives on the use of this new thing was a flop because few of the executives could imagine themselves using it. One hired a telephonist to do this.[3] The typewriter was a big hit for business offices, but still today love letters or letters of condolence are not considered socially correct if typewritten. For many years managers, usually men, would not touch the machines, thinking that such work was done by typists, usually women. Gradually, writers began to use them—even men—and many students did, too, for term papers. When personal computers first came out, many of the same people who once refused the typewriter thought the computer keyboard beneath their dignity. No more, of course: now it's just about the opposite—a noncomputer user is clearly behind the times.

We have not yet really learned how best to adapt to and use the mobile, personalized communication systems now available. Cell phone users irritate others at theaters and restaurants, they forget to recharge their batteries and lose contact in the middle of a call, or they do not recognize the restrictions such as that radio transmissions may not make it through the tall buildings downtown. By and large, younger people use these devices more than older ones and this suggests that near-universal adaptation is but a matter of time. Everett Rogers put people in five classes in terms of their willingness to adopt new ideas or systems: innovators, early adopters, early majority, late majority, and laggards.

The change in communication methods has taken some getting used to. ATMs, for example, were not universally accepted right away. Many potential users were hesitant to deal with a machine instead of the bank teller, whom they may have known personally.

The banks had to learn that once these machines went into use it was their responsibility to see to it that they worked properly and were loaded with sufficient money to take care of business until the next scheduled reload. One early adopter (a person who tends to adopt new inventions or styles quickly, ahead of most people) waited until a Friday afternoon one time to get cash for a proposed weekend trip. When he got to the ATM he found it empty of cash and by then the banks were closed until Monday. Assuring that this does not happen was part of the adaptation process for the banks. Going early, just to be sure, was part of the adaptation process for the customers who probably never considered that the bank itself would be unable to supply the weekend's cash after 4 PM on Friday.

Even something as simple as a telephone answering machine took some getting used to. At first, many people, when making a call and hearing a recorded voice inviting them to leave a message, felt as if they were on stage. Suddenly they had a microphone thrust in of their faces and were asked to talk as if to a live audience. Something similar to stage fright set in and time and again the caller simply hung up without saying anything. Today, this reaction is rare.

Cell phones became popular very quickly, but users had to learn to how to use them. Making a call was easy enough. But learning to turn a machine off so it would not ring in a theater, classroom, church, or when the owner was a guest at dinner was something else. Many have still not learned the new courtesy of telephone use.

When personal computers were made available for home use, many people could not imagine what they might do with one. The image of the computer in many minds was of a mathematical machine and few of us had need to solve differential equations in the home. Gradually, people learned that preparing income tax returns, paying bills, trading on the stock market, doing homework assignments, playing games, or keeping track of appointments, grocery lists, addresses, phone numbers, and recipes were worthwhile or fun things to do with the computer. When e-mail became available around 1980, many realized its value, and the full Internet and its World Wide Web in the 1990s added to the popularity. It is only recently that personal computers could link to the Internet without wires.

## Where Are We Today?

We have largely completed the wired city, while recognizing that not everyone enjoys all services. Figure 12.1 shows the percent of U.S. households that have telephone, radio, television, cable television, computers, and Internet connections. It can be seen that we have near total saturation of homes. Cellular telephones are sold to individuals; we have no data on how many households have at least one.

We have well-developed personal communication networks.

We have a population that has become accustomed to advanced communications technology, probably making them open to trying out yet more changes. Figure 12.2 shows the almost astonishing rate of in-crease in the annual number of e-mail messages transmitted.

Although large numbers of schools, libraries, and workplaces have Internet services available, not everyone is able to use them. Generally, those without access are the economically poorest element of society and there is some concern that this may mean a growing separation between the "haves" and "have nots" because children who grow up not knowing how to use these systems will not perform as well as others in higher school levels or on the job.

## Quality of Information

Much has been written here and elsewhere about the amount of information available to many of us and a lack of information to some of us. For those who have a lot of information the question is what does it all mean. Do we get what we *need*? Can we *trust* the messages we get? Are all our changes in technology leading to

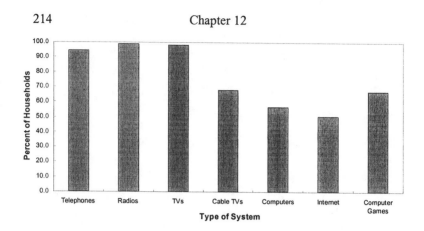

Figure 12.1. *Percent of American households having various electronic communications equipment.* Telephone, radio, and television have just about saturated American households, although the number of instruments per house keeps growing. Cable television and computers started much later but are also nearing saturation. Use of the Internet and computer games is still in the growth phase. Computer games, used for instruction as well as entertainment, are new on the scene and growing rapidly.[4]

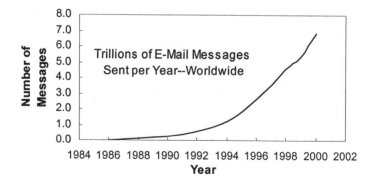

Figure 12.2. *Number of e-mail messages sent per year.* A growth curve like this is rare. The rate of increase is astounding.[5]

a better-informed public and better decisions, or do we know less and make worse decisions?

The preliminaries to the war in Iraq began in 2002, the conflict between armies ended in 2003, but resistance to the occupying Coalition forces continued long after. There was much discussion about the validity of information available to decision makers at any time. Were there weapons of mass destruction in Iraq under Saddam Hussein in 2002? If existent, were they a threat to the United States? How welcome would U.S. and allied troops be after Saddam was overthrown? Who were the people who created a resistance to the Coalition occupying force? In general, things in this war did not turn out as expected. Why? U.S. Secretary of Defense Donald Rumsfeld was quoted as saying:

> Reports that say that something hasn't happened are always interesting to me because as we know, there are known knowns; there are things we know we know. We also know there are known unknowns; that is to say we know there are some things we do not know. But there are also unknown unknowns—the ones we don't know we don't know.[6]

Much fun was poked at Mr. Rumsfeld in the press for this, but it makes perfectly good sense, if perhaps a bit overly poetic. (Not only was the quotation rewritten as fun-poking poetry, but it was even set to satirical music.) There are rather similar comments, with serious intent, in Plato,[7] amid discussions of the meaning of knowledge. Certain things almost all of us agree on; we know there are some things we do not know (Were there weapons of mass destruction in Iraq in 2002? Will it rain on our scheduled picnic next month? Am I about to marry the right person?), and most of use realize that there are surely things we don't even know the existence of, hence we cannot know that we do not know them. Regardless of one's political feelings about him, Mr. Rumsfeld has a way with words.

Daniel Boorstin put it similarly, "Education is learning what you don't even know you don't know."[8]

Perhaps we can restate this another way: Many messages come to all of us through newspapers, television news, teachers, political and religious leaders, parents, friends, acquaintances, and strangers we meet or overhear in public places. What do we accept and believe in? What do we not accept or believe in? Our basis for accepting or rejecting is our knowledge base, "things we know we know" in Mr. Rumsfeld's words. How do we get the information needed to make decisions about new information? As pointed out in chapter 6, we get it from our knowledge base and we get the information for the knowledge base from earlier information, which is a slow, painstaking process. If we are interested in monitoring the quality of nuts and bolts, we can do this with generally agreed upon measurements such as diameter, pitch of the threads, depth of the threads, or hardness and corrosion resistance of the metal. If we are evaluating intelligence reports about weapons held in a foreign country, we have to be concerned with the reliability of our source and the age of the alleged intelligence, both of which may be unknown. We must be concerned with what it is reasonable to infer from a picture of a certain kind of truck or of a radar image of incoming aircraft. Even newspapers that we had come to trust make gigantic errors at times. When information comes to us only through the World Wide Web, what do we usually know of the source?

What happens when we cannot evaluate the source of messages? We can accept it all, reject it all, or base our acceptance on something other than solid, rational, previously established facts. A consequence of this might be that people who grow up in this data-overloaded world may be so overwhelmed that they do not bother to evaluate but accept indiscriminately. The Web has been called the purest form of democracy ever developed because almost anyone can get his or her recorded thoughts out to the world. But does a flood of unevaluated and perhaps un-evaluatable messages improve democracy or debase it?

So one problem is that too much unevaluated data can lead to no evaluation, hence no quality information. In one sense this problem is caused by a lack of editorial control over content. By this is meant responsible, quality editing, which both selects material to be published and improves the clarity of expression. It means responsible people challenging the utterances of others. Without these we are left adrift.

The other side of loss of quality due to lack of editorial control is loss due to an excess of control. Today, in book and newspaper publishing and television broadcasting, there is ever-growing convergence in the organizational sense. Fewer and fewer corporations own more and more of the media of communication. Does that color or shape the news we receive? Does it color or shape the educational materials we receive? How are sensitive issues such as evolution versus creation-ism handled by textbook publishers? How about homosexuality? Who decides these questions? When a famous movie star ran for governor in California, who got the most television news coverage? What was the relationship to the motion picture industry of those networks giving him high coverage? Are we getting only the news that a few media moguls want us to get?

In our world, communication technology is making more and more messages available from more and more sources. Business practices, law, and international trade treaties are increasing the centralization of media management. Is there a happy compromise between too much control and too little? Is our paradoxical tendency toward lack of control on the Web and overcontrol of other media corrupting our degree of being informed and even knowing that we are not informed? There is no real answer except what sounds almost trite—that a public wanting to be informed must be educated, alert to manipulation, and willing to make its views heard if manipulation is suspected.

## Where Will We Be Tomorrow?

Rapid change is the single most important characteristic of communication today. Technology changes, individuals change, and organizations and societies change, each having an effect on the others. Predictions of future technology development show so much change that it is really impossible to suggest exactly how people and their organizations will change as a result. Andrew Zolli, a noted futurist, suggested that "the road to the future is paved with unintended consequences."[9]

People can invent all sorts of things. That does not mean they will be adopted. And, unexpected inventions can change society in ways never anticipated. Who, in 1945 for example, would have anticipated the impact of computers thirty years later? Changes in the size of electronic components could make for changes that we today can hardly imagine. For example, continued miniaturization could make computers small enough to be embedded in any larger machine or in a human body. In a sense, a heart pacemaker is an example. It is a machine surgically placed within a human body to regulate the rhythm of the heartbeat. What about a computer in the brain to increase memory or retain memories? What about a computer that would help us make decisions, such as which move to make in a chess or football game, or which shares to buy on the stock market, or even with whom to fall in love? What if we could detect brain waves from another person and learn to interpret them?

In strictly communication terms, we will certainly continue to see more individualized systems so we can be in contact with whomever we want, whenever we want. Messages, whether personal notes to us only or broadcasts to millions of people, could always be saved. We could walk through the ruins of Rome or Athens and transmit images to a home-bound friend, and we could do the same at a concert, ballgame, museum, or lecture. We're almost there today.

We can do some of these things now, but we can't yet go from anywhere to anywhere, as our regular mobile phones do not completely cover the earth. A much more expensive system does via satellite. Our consumer-priced, highly portable digital cameras do not have the zooming and wide-angle capabilities that professional photographic equipment has to show a panorama of scenery and then zoom in on a deer in the woods a mile away. Sometimes recording and transmission are restricted by copyright laws and while the laws might not change readily, the ease of violating them will force either change or change in the practice of protecting texts, speech, and images. This happened when dry photocopiers (the "Xerox machines" named for their first major producer) were introduced around 1960. It made copying from copyrighted material very easy, whereas it used to be difficult or expensive or both. Still, it is now possible to bring a video camera to a professional baseball game and record the action. It would be possible to transmit the images via mobile telephone. This is not legal but very hard to stop. The team and the sponsors of its broadcasts would not appreciate it.

As with changes in computers, we cannot predict exactly how people will respond to the technical changes. As we become more and more interconnected, would we be willing to give up these links, even temporarily, while on vacation? Will our families, friends, and business associates be willing for us to do that? Will there be a tendency for us to stay home more, rarely going out because we can do so much at home (or at the mountain cottage) that there is no need to show up at meetings, reunions, or even purely social occasions in person? Will that for which the term *cocooning*—wrapping ourselves in a protective cover, never going outside—has been used be a good thing? Will companies stop inventing new products because some possibly undesirable social changes might happen?

What seems likely is that the principal technical communication means is moving or has moved from telephone to radio to television to the Internet and now to hand-held devices that may soon need a name change. They are already no longer just telephones. They connect with other systems now and will connect with more in the future. Our primary communication tool will be a hand-held or pocket-held machine that will be able to handle voice transmission, radio, television, data storage, various graphic images, quality music, and printing. If we develop a means of transmitting odors, they too will pass through our little hand device. We will not need separate telephone numbers, fax numbers, mobile telephone numbers, and Internet service passwords. One will do. Our single communicator would be able to carry voice phone calls, of course, but it could also serve as a remote for television or the stereo, set the temperature in home thermostat or refrigerator, and turn off the gas while the family was in the car 200 miles away. Looking really far ahead, it might become possible to embed a communication device in our head so we would need only to think about sending a message and it would be sent. Similarly, we could receive messages, whether text, pictures, music, odors, or even touch sensations directly to our brain. Do we really want this? Most of us probably would not, but remember, we are not the people who would have such facilities made available to us. It will be our children or grandchildren who make the decision.

The increasing convergence of communication media and the increasing popularity of the Internet probably means that it will become the primary means of transmitting messages of all kinds: telephone, e-mail, which could some day replace paper mail entirely, radio and television programs, and movies for viewing in the home. Will this mean more communication than ever before? There are just so many hours in a day. What will differ is the variety of our communication.

One aspect of even today's communication is that we can receive news as it happens or very soon after. It's fun to sit in Portland, Oregon, and watch a football game in progress in New York. It's not exactly fun but sometimes irresistibly interesting to watch battles, police chases in progress, or Congress in action. But, is it true because it is timely? When the TV news shows a street demonstration for some political cause, do we see the will of the people or the will of a group of 100 people who began demonstrating only when the TV cameras showed up, and stopped as soon as they left? When we hear politicians speak, do we hear what they really think or what they think we want to hear? The point is that speed of message delivery is not necessarily related to quality of content. We are still left to judge whether or not we are seeing reality and to think about what tells us whether we are. Human judgment is still needed, not just cameras or microphones.

Another aspect of our increasing use of knowledge media of all kinds is that we are bombarded with messages, many of which are quite entertaining or almost hypnotic in their effect, especially when some major crisis is brewing or a tragedy has happened. The television coverage of the destruction of the World Trade Center on September 11, 2001, and the two recent wars in Iraq grabbed and held our attention. Yet, much of this coverage was highly repetitive. We spent a lot of time with this kind of news reporting, but we do not get much by way of explanation or critique. Daniel Boorstin pointed out that modern people could enjoy so much through newspapers, television, films, photography, art, and sound recordings that we have come to prefer the image to the reality. "The American citizen lives in a world where fantasy is more real than reality, where the image has more dignity that its original."[10] What will happen as we get still more electronic media? The book cited here was published in 1962. Boorstin possibly could not even imagine a world of picture-taking cell phones or the World Wide Web.

———————————

You, dear reader, are as good at guessing the answers to some of these questions as anyone because you will have a hand in deciding what will happen.

## Notes

1. Carr, "No Use Crying over Spilled Billions."
2. Burckhardt, *Civilization*, p. 204.
3. Drucker, "The Next Information Revolution" (Web site).
4. *Statistical Abstract of the United States* and Kurian, *Datapedia of the United States.*
5. Wilkofsky-Gruen Associates. Reported in Meadow, *Making Connections.*
6. "Department of Defense News Briefing" (Web site).
7. Plato. *Theaetatus.*
8. Boorstin, cited in http://www.brainyquote.com/quotes/authors/d/daniel_j_boorstin.html.
9. Andrew Zolli, in interview with Bill Moyers on *Now*, PBS, 2 January 2004.
10. Boorstin, *The Image*, p.37.

# Further Reading

## Wireless World

Carey et al. "Electricity Creates the Wired World."

## Global Village

McLuhan. *The Gutenberg Galaxy*, p. 31.
"Time and Space" (Web site—McLuhan on the global village).

## Convergence

Carr. "No Use Crying over Spilled Billions" (Web site).
Covell. *Digital Convergence.*
"Convergence" (Web site—McLuhan on: convergence).
Munk. *Fools Rush In.*
Negroponte. *Being Digital.*
Pitts. *Kings of Convergence.*
Thompson, "Sir, to Whom May I Direct Your Free Call" (Free telephoning on the Internet).

## Adaptation

Rogers. *Diffusion of Innovation*, 83.
*Statistical Abstract of the United States.*

## Social Impact of Media

Boorstin. *The Image.*
Star. *The Creation of the Media.*
Straubhaar and LaRose. *Media Now: Communications Media in the Information Age.*

## Future of Telecommunications

Jankowski and Fuchs. *Television Today and Tomorrow.*
Lax. *Beyond the Horizon.*

Negroponte. *Being Digital.*
Zolli. *TechTV's Catalog of Tomorrow.*

***The following are more about effects of technology change than about what changes to expect:***

Francis. *New Technology at Work.*
Friedman. *The Lexus and the Olive Tree.*
Simpson et al. *The Challenge of New Technology.*

# Bibliography

Abramson, A. 1987. *A History of Television, 1880 to 1941.* Jefferson, N. C.: McFarland.

———. 2003. *A History of Television, 1942 to 2000.* Jefferson, N.C.: McFarland & Co.

———. 1995. *Zworykin, Pioneer of Television.* Urbana: University of Illinois Press.

Aczel, A. D. 2001. *The Riddle of the Compass.* New York: Harcourt.

Adler, D. A. 1997. *Lou Gehrig: The Luckiest Man Alive.* San Diego: Harcourt Brace.

*AECMA Simplified English.* 1995. Brussels: The European Association of Aerospace Industries.

Aitken, H. G. J. 1976. *Syntony and Spark: The Origins of Radio.* New York: John Wiley & Sons.

Altmann, G. T. M. 1997. *The Ascent of Babel.* Oxford: Oxford University Press.

"Amadou Diallo Case." [cited 30 May 2004]. Available from www. washingtonpost.com/wp-dyn/nation/specials/ aroundthenation/nypd/.

*American Heritage Dictionary.* 2001. 4th ed. New York: Delta.

Angelucci, E., and A. Cucari. 1983. *Ship.* New York: Greenwich House.

Baker, M. C. 2002. *The Atoms of Language: The Mind's Hidden Rules of Grammar.* Oxford: Oxford University Press.

Behrman, C. H. 1981. *The Remarkable Writing Machine.* New York: J. Messner.

Bennett, J. A. 1987. *The Divided Circle: A History of Instruments for Astronomy, Navigation, and Surveying.* Oxford, U.K.: Phaidon.

Berg, R. E., and D. G. Stork. 1995. *The Physics of Sound.* 2nd ed. Englewood Cliffs, N.J.: Prentice Hall.

Berners-Lee, T., J. Hendler, and L. Ora. May 2001. "The Semantic Web." *Scientific American* 284(5): 34–3.

Bilby, K. M. 1986. *The General: David Sarnoff and the Rise of the Communications Industry.* New York: Harper & Row.

Billingham, J. and Pesek, R. eds. 1979. *Communication with Extraterrestrial Intellgence*. New York: Pergamon.

Bodmer, F. 1944. *The Loom of Language*. L. Hogben, ed. New York: W. W. Norton.

Boorstin, Daniel. J. 1992. *The Image: A Guide to Pseudo-Events in America*. New York: Vintage.

———. 1980. *Gresham's Law: Knowledge or Information?* Washington: The Center for the Book, Library of Congress, 1980

———. 1983. *The Discoverers: A History of Man's Search to Know His World and Himself*. New York: Random House.

Boswell, J. 1986. *James Boswell's Life of Samuel Johnson*. H. Bloom, ed. New York: Chelsea House.

*The Bowker Annual Library and Book Trade Almanac*. 2003. Medford, N.J.: Information Today.

Bradley, G. 1964. *The Story of the Pony Express*. W. F. Smith, ed. San Rafael, Calif.: Pony Express History and Art Gallery.

Brand, S. 1987. *The Media Lab*. New York: Viking Penguin.

Breuer, W. B. 1993. *Hoodwinking Hitler: The Normandy Deception*. Westport, Conn.: Praeger.

———. 2001. *Deceptions of World War II*. New York: John Wiley & Sons.

Bridges, A. "Oldest Known Photograph, Dating to 1826, to Undergo Unprecedented Scientific Analysis." March 12, 2002 [cited 24 Oct. 2004]. Available from www.dodgeglobe.com/stories/031502/nat_oldphoto.shtml.

"A Brief History of the Internet" [cited 9 Oct. 2005]. Available from www.isoc.org/internet/history/brief.shtml.

Briggs, A. 1982. *The Power of Steam: An Illustrated History of the World's Steam Age*. Chicago: University of Chicago Press.

Briggs, A., and P. Burke. 2002. *A Social History of the Media: From Gutenberg to the Internet*. Malden, Mass.: Blackwell.

Broderick, J. P. 1982. *The Able Writer: A Rhetoric and Hand Book*. New York: Harper & Row.

Brooks, J. 1976. *Telephone, the First Hundred Years*. New York: Harper & Row.

Brown, J. S., and P. Duguid. 2000. *The Social Life of Information*. Cambridge, Mass.: Harvard Business School Press.

Buckland, M. 1991. *Information and Information Systems*. New York: Praeger.

Budiansky, S. 2000. *Battle of Wits: The Complete Story of Codebreaking in World War II*. New York: Free Press.

Burckhardt, J. 1958. *The Civilization of the Renaissance in Italy*. New York: Harper & Row.

Caldwell, W. "Atlanta Telephone History" [cited 30 Sept. 2004]. Available from home.speedfactory.net/caldwell.

Campbell, D. 2002. *Technical Film and TV for Nontechnical People*. New York: Allworth.

Campbell, R., C. R. Martin, and Bettina Fabos. 2004. *Media & Culture: An Introduction to Mass Communication*. 4th ed. Boston: Bedford/St. Martin's.

Carey, J., M. Schudson, C. S. Fischer, C. Marvin, and R. Williams. 1999. "Electricity Creates the Wired World." In *Communication in History: Technology, Culture, and Society*. 3rd ed. D. Crowley and P. Heyer, eds. New York: Longman.

Carpenter, E., L. Spigel, M. Stephens, P. Aufderheide, N. Postman, and C. Paglia. 1999. "TV Times." *In Communication in History: Technology, Culture, and Society*. 3rd ed. D. Crowley and P. Heyer, eds. New York: Longman.

Carr, David. "No Use Crying over Spilled Billions." June 20, 2004. *The New York Times*, 3.

Carrington, J. F. 1969. *Talking Drums of Africa*. New York: Negro University Press.

Carter, S. 1968. *Cyrus Field: Man of Two Worlds*. New York: Putnam.

Carvalho, D. N. "Forty Centuries of Ink" [cited 19 May 2004]. Available from www.worldwideschool.org/library/books/tech/printing/FortyCenturiesofInk/chap28.html.

Casson, H. N. "Who Really Invented the Telephone?" [cited 30 Sept. 2004].Available from www.teletribute.com/the_history_of_ telephone.html.

Catania, B. "Antonio Meucci Revisited." May 7, 2003. Available from www.esanet.it/chez_basilio/index.html.

"Celebrating the 20th Anniversary." [cited 27 May 2004]. Available from motoinfo.motorola.com/motoinfo/ 20th_anniversary/documents.asp.

*Century of Flight/by the Editors of Time Life Books*. 1999. Alexandria, Va.: Time-Life Books.

Chandler, A. D., Jr. 1965. *The Railroads: The Nation's First Big Business*. New York: Harcourt, Brace and World.

Chandler, D. "Semiotics for Beginners." [cited 27 May 2004]. Available from www.aber.ac.uk/media/ Documents/S4B/semiotic.html.

————."The Transmission Model of Communication." 2000 [cited 27 May 2004]. Available from www.aber.ac.uk/media/Documents/short/trans.html.

————. 2002. *Semiotics: The Basics*. London: Routledge.

Chappell, W., and R. Bringhurst. 1999. *A Short History of the Printed Word*. 2nd ed. Vancouver, British Columbia: Hartley & Marks.

Cherry, C. 1966. *On Human Communication: A Review, a Survey, and a Criticism*. 2nd ed. Cambridge, Mass.: The MIT Press.

Chomsky, N. 1986. *Knowledge of Language: Its Nature, Origin, and Use*. New York: Praeger.

————. 2002a. *On Natural Language*. Cambridge, U.K.: Cambridge University Press.

————. 2002b. *On Nature and Language*. Cambridge, U.K.: Cambridge University Press.

————. 2002c. *The Spectacular Achievements of Propaganda*. 2nd ed. New York: Seven Stories.

Clarke, A. C. 1992. *How the World Was Won: Beyond the Global Village*. New York: Bantam.

Coe, L. 1993. *The Telegraph: A History of Morse's Invention and Its Predecessors in the United States*. Jefferson, N.C.: McFarland.

————. 1995. *The Telephone and Its Several Inventors: A History*. Jefferson, N.C.: McFarland.

————. 1996. *Wireless Radio: A Brief History*. Jefferson, N.C.: McFarland.

Cole, S. M. 1957. "Land Transport without Wheels; Roads and Bridges" In *A History of Technology*, C. Singer, E. J. Holmyard, and A. P. Hall eds. Oxford: Clarendon Press.

Congreve, W. 1967. "The Mourning Bride" In *The Complete Plays of William Congreve*. Chicago: University of Chicago Press.

"Convergence" [cited 31 May 2004]. Available from www.cios.org/encyclopedia/ mcluhan/ probe/cv/ probe_cv.html.

Coogan, J., and M. Smith. "Signal Transmission." April 28, 1999 [cited 23 May 2004]. Available from slis.cua.edu/dkb/880/lsc880/signals.htm.

Corballis, M. C. 2003. *From Hand to Mouth*. Princeton: Princeton University Press.

Coren, S. 2000. *How to Speak Dog*. New York: Fireside.

Covell, A. 2000. *Digital Convergence*. Newport, R.I.: Aegis.

Cringley, R. X. "Digital TV: A Cringely Crash Course" [cited 26 May 2004]. Available from www.pbs.org/ opb/crashcourse/.

Crowley, D., and P. Heyer. 1998. *Communication in History: Technology, Culture, and Society.* 3rd ed. New York: Longman.

Cullinan, G. 1973. *The United States Postal Service.* New York: Praeger.

"D-Day" [cited 28 May 2004]. Available from www.worldwar2history. info/D-Day/.

Dana, P. H. "Global Positioning System Overview." 2000 [cited 19 Oct. 2004]. Available from www.colorado.edu/geography/gcraft/notes/gps/ gps.html.

Daniels, D., and B. Daniels. 1991. *English Grammar.* New York: Harper-Collins.

"Department of Defense News Briefing—Secretary Rumsfeld and General Myers." February 12, 2002 [cited 2 June 2004]. Available from www.defenselink.mil/news/Feb2002/t02122002_t212sdv2.html.

Dern, D. P. 1994. *The Internet Guide for New Users.* New York: McGraw-Hill.

"Detective: Bullets Fell From Diallo's Body As It Was Lifted From Scene." February 2, 2000 [cited 18 Oct 2004]. Available from www.cnn.com/ 2000/US/02/02/diallo.trial.02/.

Devlin, K. J. 1999. *Infosense: Understanding Information in the Knowledge Society.* New York: W. H. Freeman.

"Directory of Notable Photographers." [cited 29 June 2004]. Available fromphotography.about.com/library/dop/bldop_ldague.htm?once= true&.

"Disorders of Muscle Stimulation." In *The Merck Manual of Medical Information.* R. Berkow, ed. 1997.Whitehouse Station, N.J.: Merck Research Laboratories.

Dominick, J. R. 2002. *The Dynamics of Mass Communication: Media in the Digital Age.* 7th ed. Boston: McGraw-Hill.

Domjan, M., and J. W. Grau. 2003. *The Principles of Learning and Behavior.* 5th ed. Belmont, Cal.: Wadsworth.

Drucker, P. F. "The Next Information Revolution." August 24, 1998 [cited 14 Oct. 004]. Available from www.versaggi.net/ecommerce/ articles/drucker-inforevolt.htm.

Durham, M. G., and Kellner, Douglas M. 2001. *Media and Cultural Studies.* Malden, Mass.: Blackwell

"'Earliest Writing' Found." May 4, 1999 [cited 18 Oct. 2004]. Available from news.bbc.co.uk/1/hi/sci/tech/334517.stm.

Eisenstein, E. L. 1979. *The Printing Press As an Agent of Change.* London: Cambridge University Press.

"Electromagnetic Spectrum." [cited 26 May 2004]. Available from imagine.gsfc.nasa.gov/docs/science/ know_11/emspectrum.html.

Elisseeff, V., ed. 2000. *The Silk Roads: Highways of Culture and Commerce.* Paris: UNESCO: New York: Berghahn Books.

Ellul, J. 1965. *Propaganda.* New York: Alfred A. Knopf.

Fang, I. 1997. *A History of Mass Communication: Six Information Revolutions.* Boston: Focal.

"Fax Technology—Testing Issues" [cited 28 April 2004]. Available from www.iec.org/online/tutorials/faxtech_test/ topic04.html.

Finamore, D., ed. 2004. *Maritime History As World History.* Gainsville, Fla.: University Press of Florida; Salem, Mass.: Peabody Essex Museum.

Finley, C. 1997. *Printing Paper and Ink.* Albany, New York: Delmar.

"First Alphabet Found in Egypt." May 14, 2004 Available from www. archaeology. \org/0001/newsbriefs/egypt.html.

Fisher, D. E., and M. J. Fisher. 1995. *Tube: The Invention of Television.* Washington: Counterpoint.

Fox, C., W. Frakes, and P. Gandel. 1988. "Foundational Issues in Knowledge-Based Information Systems." *The Canadian Journal of Information Science* 13(3/4): 90–102.

Francis, A. 1986. *New Technology at Work.* Oxford: Clarendon.

"The FreeDictionary.Com." 2004 [cited 19 Oct. 2004]. Available from www.computerdictionary. thefreedictionary.com/.

Friedman, T. L. 2000. *The Lexus and the Olive Tree.* New York: Anchor Books.

Geldard, F. A. 1972. *The Human Senses.* New York: John Wiley & Sons.

Gerbarg, D., ed. 1999. *The Economics, Technology, and Content of Digital TV.* Boston: Kluwer.

Goodwin, A., and G. Whannel, eds. 1990. *Understanding Television.* London and New York: Routledge.

Green, J. A. 1997. *Electromagnetic Radiation: Fundamentals and Applications.* Wichita, Kans.: Greenwood Research.

Grosvenor, E. S., and M. Wesson. 1997. *Alexander Graham Bell: The Life and Times of the Man Who Invented the Telephone.* New York: Harry Abrams.

Hall, E. T. 1959. *The Silent Language.* Westport, Conn.: Greenwood.

Hamilton, E. 1942. *Mythology: Timeless Tales of Gods and Heroes.* New York: New American Library.

Harriss, J., K. Leiter, and S. Johnson. 1985. *The Complete Reporter: Fundamentals of News Gathering, Writing, and Editing*. 5th ed. New York: Macmillan.

Hayakawa, S. I., and A. R. Hayakawa. 1990. *Language in Thought and Action*. 5th ed. San Diego: International Thomson.

Hecht, J. 1999. *City of Light: The Story of Fiber Optics*. New York: Oxford University Press.

Heyerdahl, T. 1980. *Early Man and the Ocean: A Search for the Beginnings of Navigation and Seaborne Civilizations*. New York: Vintage.

Hirsch, R. 2000. *Seizing the Light: A History of Photography*. Boston: McGraw-Hill.

*Historical Statistics of the United States, Colonial Times to 1970, Part 2*. 1975. Washington D.C.: U.S. Department of Commerce.

"History of the Silk Road." 2004 [cited 26 May 2004]. Available from www.travelchinaguide.com/silkroad/history.

Hudson, H. E. 1990. *Communication Satellites: Their Development and Impact*. New York: Free Press.

Hunter, D. 1978. *Papermaking: The History and Technique of an Ancient Craft*. New York: Dover.

*Hyperdictionary*. 2003 [cited 18 Oct 2004]. Available from www. hyperdictionary.com.

Ifrah, G. 1985. *From One to Zero: A Universal History of Numbers*. New York: Viking Penguin.

Illich, I. 1993. *In the Vineyard of the Text*. Chicago: University of Chicago Press.

Innis, H. 1986. *Empire and Communications*. Victoria, B.C.: Press Porcepic Limited.

"The Integrated Circuit." 2004 [cited 27 May 2004]. Available from nobel.se/physics/educational/ integrated_circuit/history/.

Irons, W. 2001. "Religion as a Hard-to-Fake Sign of Commitment." In *Evolution and the Capacity for Commitment*. R. Nesse, ed. 292–309. New York: Russell Sage Foundation.

Jamieson, K. H., and K. K. Campbell. 2001. *The Interplay of Influence: News, Advertising, Politics, and the Mass Media*. 5th ed. Belmont, Calif.: Wadsworth.

Jankowski, G. F., and D. C. Fuchs. 1995. *Television Today and Tomorrow*. New York: Oxford University Press.

Jian, G. "Organizational Knowledge and Learning—A Speculation, Review, and Critique." 2000 [cited 30 May 2004]. Available from www.colorado.edu/communication/meta-discourses/Papers/Jian_ knowledge.htm#model.

"Johann Philipp Reis." 2004 [cited 17 Sept. 2004]. Available from german.about.com/library/blerf_reis.htm.

Johansen, J. "History of Navigation." 2001 [cited 25 May 2004]. Available from www.pip.dknet.dk/~pip261/ navigation.html.

Katz, E. "Johann Philipp Reis." [cited 22 Aug 2004]. Available from chem.ch.huji.ac.il/~eugeniik/history/reis. html.

Keegan, J. 2003. *Intelligence in War: Knowledge of the Enemy From Napoleon to Al-Qaeda*. New York: Alfred A. Knopf.

Kern, S., S. Eyman, S. J. Douglas, W. Stott, C. Sterling, J. M. Kittross, and M. McLuhan. 1999. "Radio Days." In *Communication in History: Technology, Culture, and Society*. D. Crowley and P. Heyer, eds. 213–57. 3rd ed. New York: Longman.

Kilgour, F. G. 1998. *The Evolution of the Book*. Oxford and New York: Oxford Univesity Press.

Knight, D. C. 1960. *The First Book of Sound: A Basic Guide to the Science of Acoustics*. New York: Franklin Watts.

Kurian, George T., ed. 2001. *Datapedia of the United States, 1790-2005*, 2nd ed. Lanham, Md. Bernian Press

Landstrom, B. 1961. *The Ship, an Illustrated History*. Garden City, N.Y.: Doubleday.

Langford, M. J. 1980. *The Story of Photography from Its Beginnings to the Present Day*. London and New York: Focal.

Lavine, J. M., and D. B. Wackman. 1988. *Managing Media Organizations: Effective Leadership of the Media*. New York: Longman.

Lax, S. 1997. *Beyond the Horizon: Communications Technologies Past, Present and Future*. Luton, U.K.: University of Luton Press.

Lee, J. A. N., S. Winkler, and M. Smith"Key Events in the History of Computing." [cited 24 Oct 2004]. Available from ei.cs.vt.edu/ ~history/50th/30.minute.show.html.

Lee, W. C. Y. 1989. *Mobile Cellular Telecommunications Systems*. New York: McGraw-Hill.

Lenhoff, H. M., P. P. Wang, F. Greenberg, and U. Bellugi. December 1997. "Williams Syndrome and the Brain." *Scientific American* 276(6): 68–73.

Lerner, E. J. August 1999. "Communicating Via Brain Waves." *The Industrial Physicist*: 14–16.

Lewis, T. 1993. *Empire of the Air*. New York: HarperPerennial.

Linoff, V. M. 2000. *The Typewriter: An Illustrated History*. Mineola, N.Y.: Dover.

Logan, R. K. 1986. *The Alphabet Effect*. New York: William Morrow.

———. 1995. *The Fifth Language*. Toronto: Stoddard.

Mackay, A. 1972. *A Collection of Ancient Piobaireachd or Highland Pipe Music*. East Ardsley, U.K.: EP Publishing Ltd.

Macksey, K. 2003. *The Searchers: How Radio Interception Changes the Course of Both World Wars*. London: Cassell.

"Mad Man Muntz." [cited 26 May 2004]. Available from www.smecc.org/mad_man_muntz!.htm.

Man, J. 2000. *Alpha Beta: How 26 Letters Shaped the Western World*. New York: John Wiley & Sons.

Manguel, A. 1996. *A History of Reading*. New York: Viking Penguin.

Marchionini, G. 1995. *Information Seeking in Electronic Environments*. Cambridge, U.K. and New York: Cambridge University Press.

Mares, G. C. 1985. *The History of the Typewriter: Successor to the Pen*. Arcadia, Calif.: Post-Era Books.

Marsden, B. 2002. *Watt's Perfect Engine: Steam and the Age of Invention*. Cambridge, U.K.: Icon.

Marshack, A. 1991. *The Roots of Civilization*. Mt. Kisco, N.Y.: Moyer Bell Limited.

———. 1999. "The Art and Symbols of Ice Age Man." *In Communication in History: Technology, Culture, and Society*. 3rd ed. D. Crowley and P. Heyer, eds. 5–14. New York: Longman.

McLuhan, M. 1994. *Understanding Media, the Extensions of Man*. Cambridge: The MIT Press.

———. 1995. *The Gutenberg Galaxy*. Toronto: University of Toronto Press.

McLuhan, M. and Quentin Fiore. 1967. *The Medium Is the Massage: An Inventory of Effects*. New York: Bantam Books. Reprinted: 1989. New York: Touchstone Books.

McShane, C. 1997. *The Automobile: A Chronology of Its Antecedents, Development, and Impact*. Westport, Conn.: Greenwood.

Meadow, C. T. 1998. *Ink into Bits: A Web of Converging Media*. Lanham, Md.: Scarecrow.

———. 2002. *Making Connections: Communication Through the Ages*. Lanham, Md.: Scarecrow Press.

Meadow, C. T., B. R. Boyce, and D. H. Kraft. 2000. *Text Information Retrieval Systems*. 2nd ed. San Diego: Academic.

*Merriam-Webster Online Dictionary*. 2004 [cited 14 Oct. 2004]. Available from www.m-w.com/cgi-bin/dictionary?book=Dictionary&va=lexical +meaning.

Minow, N. "Wasteland Speech Holds True after All These Years." May 9, 1961 [cited 11 August 2004]. Available from www.janda.org/b20/ News%20articles/vastwastland.htm.

Minsky, M. 1985. "Communication with Alien Intelligence." In *Extraterrestrials: Science and Alien Intelligence*. E. Regis, ed. Cambridge: Cam-bridge University Press.

*The Mishnah*. 1933. H. Danby, Trans. Oxford: Oxford University Press.

Mitchell, B. R. 1998. *International Historical Statistics: The Americas 1750–1993*. New York: Stockton Press.

Morris, D. 1994. *Bodytalk: A World Guide to Gestures*. London: Jonathan Cape.

Morris, D., P. Collett, P. Marsh, and M. O'Shaughnessy. 1979. *Gestures, Their Origins and Distribution*. New York: Stein and Day.

Mumford, L., E. L. Eisenstein, W. Ong, H. J. Graff, J. B. Thompson, and R. Darnton. "The Print Revolution." In *Communication in History: Technology, Culture, and Society*. 3rd ed. 1999. D. Crowley and P. Heyer, eds. 85–134. New York: Longman.

Munk, N. 2004. *Fools Rush In: Steve Case, Jerry Levin, and the Unmaking of AOL Time Warner*. New York: Harper Business.

"Navigational Instruments" [cited 26 May 2004]. Available from www.celestialnavigation.net/instruments.html.

"Nebraska K-12 Reading/Writing Framework." 1999 [cited 30 May 2004]. Available from www.nde.state.ne.us/READ/FRAMEWORK/ strand4/index.html.

Negroponte, N. 1995. *Being Digital*. New York: Alfred A. Knopf.

Neeld, Elizabeth Cowan. 1990. *Writing*. Glenview, Ill.: Scott, Foresman/Little, Brown Higher Education.

Nevins, A., and H. S. Commager. 1966. *A Short History of the United States*. 5th ed. New York: Alfred A. Knopf.

Newsom, D., and J. A. Wollert. 1988. *Media Writing: Preparing Information for the Mass Media*. 2nd ed. Belmont, Calif.: Wadsworth.

Nieh, J. C. October 1999. "Stingless-Bee Communication." *American Scientist* 87(5).

"NTSC Turorials, Free." 2003 [cited 30 May 2004]. Available from ntsc-tv.com.

Nunberg, G. 1996. *The Future of the Book*. Berkeley, Calif.: University of California Press.

O'Donnell, L. B., P. Benoit, and C. Hausman. 1986. *Modern Radio Production*. 2nd ed. Belmont, Cal.: Wadsworth.

Ogden, F. 1993. *The Last Book You'll Ever Read*. Toronto: Macfarlane, Walter & Ross.

Ong, W. 1999. "Orality, Literacy, and Modern Media." In *Communication in History: Technology, Culture, and Society*. 3rd ed. D. Crowley and P. Heyer, eds. pp. 60–7. New York: Longman.

Oslin, G. P. 1992. *The Story of Telecommunications*. Macon, Ga.: Mercer University Press.

"Our History." 2004 [cited 27 May 2004]. Available from intelsat.com/aboutus/ourhistory/index.aspx.

*Oxford English Dictionary*, 2nd ed. 1989. Simpson, J. A. and E. S. C. Weiner. New York: Oxford University Press /Oxford: Clarendon Press.

Parker, I. January 20, 2003. "Reading Minds." *The New Yorker*, 52–63.

Penzias, A. 1989. *Ideas and Information*. New York: Simon & Schuster Touchstone.

Pierce, J. R. 1968. *The Beginnings of Satellite Communications*. San Francisco: San Francisco Press.

———. 1974. *Almost All About Waves*. Cambridge, Mass.: The MIT Press.

Pinker, S. 1995. *The Language Instinct*. New York: HarperPerennial.

———. 1999. *Words and Rules: The Ingredients of Language*. New York: Basic.

Pitts, G. 2002. *Kings of Convergence: The Fight for Control of Canada's Media*. Toronto: Doubleday Canada.

Plato. 1986. *Phaedrus*. C. J. Rowe, trans. Warminster, U.K.: Aris & Phillips.

———. *Theaetatus*. 1987. R. M. H. Waterfield, trans. New York: Viking Penguin.

Pollan, M. 2001. *The Botany of Desire*. New York: Random House.

Polo, M. 1958. *The Travels*. R. Latham, trans. New York: Penguin Books.

Pool, I. de S. 1977. *The Social Impact of the Telephone*. Cambridge, Mass.: The MIT Press.

Pratkanis, A., and E. Aronson. 2001. *Age of Propaganda: The Everyday Uses of Persuasion*. New York: W. H. Freeman.

Randier, J. 1980. *Marine Navigation Instruments*. John E. Powell, trans. London: J. Murray.

Reid, T. R. 2001. *The Chip: How Two Americans Invented the Microchip and Launched a Revolution*. New York: Random House.

Rich, F. "Napster Runs for President in '04." December 21, 2003 [cited 27 Dec. 2003]. Available from www.nytimes.com/2003/12/21/arts/ 21RICH.html?pagewanted=all&position=.

Richards, I. A., and C. K. Ogden. 1989. *The Meaning of Meaning: A Study of the Influence of Language Upon Thought and the Science of Symbolism.* San Diego: Harcourt, Brace & Jovanovich.

Riordan, M., and L. Hoddeson. 1997. *Crystal Fire: The Invention of the Transistor and the Birth of the Information Age.* New York: W. W. Norton & Co.

Ritz, T., S. Adem, and K. Schulten. 2000. "A Model for Photorecep- tor-Based Magnetoreception in Birds." *Biophysical Journal* 78(2): 707–18.

Ritz, T., and K. Schulten. "The Magnetic Sense of Animals." March 8, 2004 [cited 29 May 2004]. Available from ks.uiuc.edu/Research/ magsense/.

Robbins, M. 1998. *The Railway Age.* 3rd ed. New York: St. Martin's.

Robinson, A. 1999. "The Origins of Writing." In *Communication in History: Technology, Culture, and Society.* 3rd ed. D. Crowley and P. Heyer, eds. pp. 36–42. New York: Longman.

Roddy, D. 2001. *Satellite Communications.* 3rd ed. New York: McGraw-Hill.

Rogers, E. 1995. *Diffusion of Innovation.* 4th ed. New York: Free Press.

Rosenman, S. I. 1952. *Working with Roosevelt.* New York: Harper.

Rosner, S. R. 2002. *Understanding Williams Syndrome: Behavioral Patterns and Intervention.* Mahwah, N. J.: L. Earlbaum.

Ruhlen, M. 1996. *The Origin of Language: Tracing the Evolution of the Mother Tongue.* New York: John Wiley & Sons.

Rutherford, P. 2000. *Endless Propaganda: The Advertising of Public Goods.* Toronto and Buffalo, N.Y.: University of Toronto Press.

Sacks, D. 2003. *Language Visible.* New York: Broadway Books.

Sagan, C. 2000. *Carl Sagan's Cosmic Connection: An Extraterrestrial Perspective.* Cambridge, U. K. and New York: Cambridge University Press.

Schmandt-Besserat, D. 1996. *How Writing Came About.* First abridged ed. Austin: University of Texas Press.

———. 1999. "The Earliest Precursor of Writing." In *Communication in History: Technology, Culture, and Society.* 3rd ed. D. Crowley and P. Heyer, eds. pp. 15–23. New York: Longman.

Schneider, P. January 30, 2003. Charlie Rose television interview. Public Broadcasting System, Washington, D.C.

Schwartz, E. I. 2002. *Last Lone Inventor: A Tale of Genius, Deceit, and the Birth of Television.* New York: Harper Collins.

Schwartz, M. 1990. *Information Transmission, Modulation and Noise.* 4th ed. New York: McGraw-Hill.

Sebeok, T. A., ed. 1977. *How Animals Communicate.* Bloomington: Indiana University Press.

———. 1994. *Signs: An Introduction to Semiotics.* Toronto and Buffalo: University of Toronto Press.

Sellen, A. J., and R. H. R. Harper. 2002. *The Myth of the Paperless Office.* Cambridge, Mass.: The MIT Press.

Shannon, C. E., and W. Weaver. 1959. *The Mathematical Theory of Communication.* Urbana: University of Illinois Press.

Sherman, W. T. 1990. *Memoirs of General William T. Sherman.* New York: Literary Classics of the United States.

Shlain, L. 1998. *The Alphabet Versus the Goddess.* New York: Viking.

Shostak, S., and A. Barnett. 2003. *Cosmic Company: The Search for Life in the Universe.* Cambridge, U. K. and New York: Cambridge University Press.

Silverman, K. 2003. *Lightning Man: The Accursed Life of Samuel F.B. Morse.* New York: Alfred A. Knopf.

Simpson, D., J. Love, and J. Walker. 1987. *The Challenge of New Technology.* Boulder, Colo.: Westview.

Singer, C. J., J. Holmyard, A. R. Hall, and T. I. Williams, eds. 1954–1958. *A History of Technology.* 8 vols. Oxford: Oxford University Press.

Smith, C. 1995. *The Storytellers: From Mel Allen to Bob Costas: Sixty Years of Baseball From the Broadcast Booth.* New York: Macmillan.

Smith, C. U. M. 2001. *Biology of Sensory Systems.* Chichester, U.K. and New York: John Wiley & Sons.

Smithsonian Institution, and National Air and Space Museum. 1989. *Milestones of Aviation.* J. T. Greenwood, ed. New York: Hugh Lauter Assoc.

Sobel, D. 1995. *Longitude.* New York: Walker.

Solymar, L. 1999. *Getting the Message: A History of Communications.* Oxford: Oxford University Press.

Sosis, R. March-April 2004. "The Adaptive Value of Religious Ritual." *American Scientist* 92(2): 166–72.

Standage, T. 1998. *The Victorian Internet.* New York: Berkeley.

Star, P. 2004. *The Creation of the Media.* New York: Basic.

*Statistical Abstract of the United States.* 123rd ed. 2003. Washington D.C.: U.S. Department of Commerce.

Steinbock, D. 2003. *Wireless Horizon: Strategy and Competition in the Worldwide Marketplace*. New York: AMACOM.

Sterling, C. H., and G. Shiers. 2000. *History of Telecommunications Technology: An Annotated Bibliography*. Lanham, Md.: Scarecrow.

Straubhaar, J. D., and R. LaRose. 2002. *Media Now: Communications Media in the Information Age*. 4th ed. Belmont, Calif.: Thomson/Wadsworth.

Swift, D. W. 1990. *SETI Pioneers: Scientists Talk About Their Search for Extraterrestrial Intelligence*. Tucson: University of Arizona Press.

Thompson, Nicholas. October 12, 2003. "Sir, to Whom May I Direct Your Free Call?" *The New York Times*, 3.

Thoreau, H. D. 1951. *Walden*. New York: Bramhall House.

"Time and Space." [cited 31 May 2004]. Available from www.cios.org/encyclopedia/mcluhan/probe/ts/ probe_ts.html.

"A Timeline History of the IBM Typewriter." July 31, 2003 [cited 26 May 2004]. Available from www. etypewriters.com/history.htm.

Tooley, R. V. 1970. *Maps and Map-Makers*. New York: Crown.

"The Transistor." 2004 [cited 27 May 2004]. Available from www.nobel. se/ physics/educational/transistor/ history/index.html.

"Transistorized!" 1999 [cited 27 May 2004]. Available from www.pbs.org/transistor/album1/.

"TV Screens." [cited 26 May 2004]. Available from www. colorado.edu/physics/2000/tv/big_picture.html.

Twain, M. "The First Writing Machines." 2003 [cited 23 May 2004]. Available from www.online-literature. com/twain/318/.

Ullman, B. L. 1989. *Ancient Writing and Its Influence*. Toronto: University of Toronto Press.

UNESCO Statistical Yearbook. 1999. Paris: UNESCO.

U.S. Congress. House. HR 269. 107th Cong.

Vickers, A. August 1, 2003. "Opening Address." Sooke ( British Columbia) Fine Arts 2003. Speech.

"A Visit with Hall of Famer Ted Williams." [cited 27 May 2004]. Available from www.baseballhalloffame.org/history/Q_A/Q_A_williams_ted.htm.

Vivian, J. 2003. *The Media of Mass Communication 2003 Update*. Boston: Pearson/Allyn & Bacon.

von Frisch, K. 1967. *The Dance Language and Orientation of Bees*. Cambridge, Mass.: Belknap.

Walker, M. M., T. E. Denis, and J. L. Kirschvink. December 2002. "The Magnetic Sense and Its Use in Long Distance Navigation by Animals." *Current Opinion in Neurobiology* 12(6): 735–44.

Warner, J. 1994. *From Writing to Computers*. London and New York: Routledge.

———. 2001. *Information, Knowledge, Text*. Lanham, Md.: Scarecrow.

Weaver, W. 1959. "Some Recent Contributions to the Mathematical Theory of Communication." In *The Mathematical Theory of Communication*, 95-117. Urbana: The University of Illinois Press.

———. 1959. "Some Recent Contributions, 2.5 Noise." In *The Mathematical Theory of Communication*, 108–12. Urbana, Ill.: The University of Illinois Press.

*Webster's New World Dictionary of the American Language*. 3rd ed. 1998. New York: Webster's New World.

*Webster's Third New International Dictionary of the English Language, Unabridged*. 2002. Springfield, Mass.: Merriam-Webster.

Weightman, G. 2003. *Signor Marconi: How an Amateur Inventor Defied Scientists and Began a Revolution*. London: HarperCollins.

Wilford, John N. 9 Nov. 2005. "A Us for Ancient, Describing an Alphabet Found Near Jerusalem" *The New York Times*, [cited 12 Nov. 2005] www.nytimes,com/2005/11/09/international/middleeast/09alphabet.html.

———. 6 April 1999 "Who Began Writing? Many Theories, Few Answers." *The New York Times*, [cited 27 Feb. 2005] www.english.uga.edu/~hypertext/040699sci-early-writing.html.

Wiggins, R. W. 1994. *The Internet for Everyone: A Guide for Users and Providers*. New York, Inc.: McGraw-Hill.

Williams, Robert V. and Ben-Ami Lipetz. 2005. *Covert and Overt*. Medford, N.J.: Information Today.

"Williams Syndrome Association." 2004 [cited 30 May 2004]. Available from www.williams-syndrome.org/ forteachers/teachers.html.

Winston, B. 1998. *Media Technology and Society: A History From the Telegraph to the Internet*. London ; New York: Routledge.

Wittgenstein, Ludwig. 1958. *Philosophical Investigations*, 2nd ed. G. E. M. Anscombe, trans. Oxford, U.K. and Malden, Mass.: Blackwell.

*WordIQ Dictionary*. 2004 [cited 1 Oct. 2005]. Available from www.wordiq.com/definition/Information.

"World: America's Police Shoot At Unarmed Man 41 Times." February 8, 1999 [cited 30 May 2004]. Available from news.bbc.co.uk/1/hi/world/americas/273666.stm.

Bibliography

Yule, G. 1985. *The Study of Language*. Cambridge, U. K.: Cambridge University Press.

Zakon, R. H. "Hobbes' Internet Timeline V7.0." 2004 Available from www.zakon.org/robert/internet/timeline/.

Zolli, A. January 2, 2004. Interview with Bill Moyers on *Now*. Public Broadcasting System, Washington, D.C.

Zolli, A., ed. 2003. *TechTV's Catalog of Tomorrow*. Indianapolis, Ind.: Que Publishing.

# Index

adaptation, 210–13
Advanced Research Projects Agency, 80–81
AECMA. *See* European Association of Aerospace Industries
aircraft: invention of, 39–40; trans-Atlantic flight by, 40
Akkadia, 11
Alexandria, library of, 117
alphabet, development of, 10–14
ALS. *See* amyotrophic lateral sclerosis
Amalek, 12
ambiguity, value of, 153
America Online (AOL), 209
American Telephone & Telegraph Co., 57, 209
American Sign Language, 131
amyotrophic lateral sclerosis, 181
animals as communication channels, 31–33, 139
Archer, Frederick, 46
ARPA. *See* Advanced Research Projects Agency
ARPANet, 80–82
AT&T. *See* American Telephone & Telegraph Co.
Atlantic Ocean: crossing of, by air, 40; telegraph cable across, 52
automatic teller machines (ATM), 203, 211

automobile: invention of, 37–39; as a channel of communication, 37

Babylon, communication with captives in, 119–20
Baird, James, 69–70, 72–73
BBC. *See* British Broadcasting Corp.
balloons, aerial, 39–40
bandwidth, 65
Bardeen, John, 76
BASIC computer language, 131
bee communication, 139
Belgium, multiple languages in, 132
Bell, Alexander Graham, 2, 53–54
Bell Laboratories, 77–78, 83
Berlat, Norman, 12
Bernstein, Leonard, 141
Bessarion, Cardinal, 210
Betamax, 89
Bible, 3, 8, 11
boats and ships, as communication channels, 31–34, 201–2
books: impact of printed, 210; publication of, 18, 157–58
Boorstin, Daniel, 215, 221
brain disorders, 179–81
Braun, Karl, 70
British Broadcasting Corp., 69–70
Brittain, Walter, 76

# About the Author

Charles T. Meadow is professor emeritus, Faculty of Information Studies, University of Toronto where he previously served as associate dean. He has been a professor at Drexel University; visiting professor at the University of North Carolina at Chapel Hill, University of Washington, University of the West Indies, and University of Sheffield.

He is a member of the American Society for Information Science and Technology and had served as editor, *Journal of the American Society for Information Science* from 1976 to 1984. As a member of the Canadian Association for Information Science he was editor of the *Canadian Journal of Information Science*, 1985 to 1986, publications director, 1986 to 1994, president, 1994, and past president, 1995.

Professor Meadow was awarded Honorable Mention by the New York Academy of Science Children's Science Book Awards in 1975; the Research Award of the American Society for Information Science in 1995, and was the recipient, with co-authors, of the society's Information Science Book of the Year award in 2000. He received the NJ/ASIS Distinguished Lectureship Award from the New Jersey Chapter of the American Society for Information Science in 1986, and was twice a Sam Lazerow Lecturer, at Columbia University in 1986 and at Drexel University in 1988. He is listed in *Canadian Who's Who*, Marquis' *Who's Who in America* and *Who's Who in Science and Engineering*.

Previous book publications include: *Making Connections: Communications through the Ages*; *Text Information Retrieval Systems*, 2nd ed. (with Bert Boyce and Donald Kraft); *Ink into Bits: A Web of Converging Media*; *Measurement in Information Science* (with Bert Boyce and Donald Kraft); *Telecommunications for Management* (with Albert S. Tedesco); *Basics of Online Searching* (with Pauline Cochrane); *Applied Data Management, Sounds and Signals: How We Communicate; The Analysis of Information Systems; Man-Machine Communication;* and *The Story of Computers*.